French Phrasebook

1400+ Essential French Phrases and Expressions to Build Your Confidence in Speaking French

Also available:
French Slang Essentials: All The Essential French Slang You Need to Speak
Like A Native
French Crash Course: A Seven-Day Guide to Learning Basic French (with
audio)

For more products by Frédéric BIBARD/Talk in French, visit
https://www.amazon.com/Frederic-BIBARD (for US)
https://www.amazon.co.uk/Frederic-BIBARD (for UK)
Or go to https://store.talkinfrench.com.

Introduction

*T*ravelling to France, or any French-speaking country, can be quite daunting. I'm sure you've heard some terrible things about being a tourist in France, like how haughty waiters ignore your orders, or how French people, especially the Parisians, can be just downright rude and unwilling to help tourists. As a French man who spends a lot of time talking to foreigners, I've heard this all before. And though I know how travelling in France can be a bittersweet experience,I believe this is just a general misunderstanding that can be fixed by two things:

1. Better communication

2. A background on French culture

You would be amazed at how a simple « Bonjour », « merci », or « s'il vous plait » can be a game changer when dealing with sales clerks, waiters or any French person on the street. Even if you're able to communicate just a tiny bit in French, I guarantee that you will have a totally different experience in my country.

Such is the reason that I created this book: to help address those two things I mentioned above. With this book, I want to make your travelling experience in France as smooth as possible by giving you all the

Introduction

phrases and vocabulary you need to communicate in French in a simple way.

But just to be clear: this book will not teach you French. Instead, it is designed to serve as a great guide to help you find your way through all the possible scenarios as a tourist in France. It will help you know the right words to say from the moment you arrive at the airport, to sightseeing, shopping, dining, and even during emergencies.

I have also included bonus material to give you a background on French culture, as well as to make dining in France a very pleasant experience.

Here's what you'll find inside:

- 1,400+ French words and expressions with English translations. This includes an easy phonetic pronunciation guide. (e.g. bonjour = bon·zhoor)

- A menu reader to help you order the right food. Refer to 600+ food vocabulary and French dishes translated from French to English.

- A pronunciation guide

- A mini-guide of cultural differences

Aside from tourists, this book would also benefit those who wish to jumpstart their French language lessons. If you are a beginner level learner, or you have previously studied French before and would like to review some basic phrases, this book is also great for you.

I hope you'll enjoy this book.

Merci, Thank you.

Frédéric BIBARD
Founder, Talk in French

Advice on how to use this book effectively

*T*ake this book with you when you travel to France, and see how your level of confidence would greatly improve.

This book is arranged according to theme in order to make searching easier for you. Whatever scenario you find yourself in, just flip over to that page and take a look at the list of phrases listed. The first column contains the English phrase, the second column is for the French translation of the phrase, and the third column is the easy phonetic pronunciation guide.

If you wish to practice for better pronunciation, or train your ears to listen to French as spoken by native speakers, you might want to get the FULL VERSION of this book, which comes with 89 minutes of audio for pronunciation and listening practice, as well as several other bonus materials. You can get it here.

Contents

Contents

Contents

Contents

Contents

Contents

Important: The link to download the MP3s is available at the end of this eBook.

Chapter 0 :
Mastering Pronunciation

How to pronounce French the right way

(Optional): You can obtain the MP3s for the pronunciation guide by downloading the Free French Language Package:

http://www.talkinfrench.com/french-free-package

*T*here is a charming quality to the spoken French language that most people find utterly delightful. The way in which the words seem to melt together to form pleasant sounds and flowing melodic tones can be both enchanting and intimidating at the same time. It is enchanting enough for those who are not French to strive to replicate its romantic-sounding inflections, but very intimidating when you listen to French people actually speak.

No need to get intimidated for long, though. By choosing this guide, you are already on the right track for learning how to speak French because this discussion is solely focused on proper French pronunciation. Whether you are beginning to learn the language or you simply need to brush up on your intonation, this is the perfect tool for you to refer to!

The study method and guide presented below are formulated for English speakers and will help you to grasp the pronunciation rules better. It can be tricky for newbie learners, but with regular practice in speaking and reading, you should be able to do quite well soon enough. Remember, you do not need to memorize these rules; by referring to this guide consistently, you will improve in no time. So study it as often as you'd like! It will be ingrained in your mind before you know it.

Here is a tip from a native French speaker (aka me):

Don't be too hard on yourself when you can't fully grasp the pronunciation rules after a few hours of practice. It takes time to learn how to pronounce French words properly – months, in fact. Besides, it's extremely rare to see a foreigner with 100% correct pronunciation. But does it really matter? France is a hugely multicultural country and the French people are quite familiar (and accepting!) with a wide range of accents. So don't beat yourself to a pulp, and just keep practising until you start to pull off French quite nicely.

So are you ready?

Here we go!

PART 1. THE STRESS
(and why you shouldn't
stress it out)

When compared to the English language, French has a more distinct sound and a flat intonation. The stress is mostly even except for the last syllable, which is given a bit more emphasis. Check out the following example using the word 'important'.

Notice the difference in stress between the English and French pronunciations:

English: im-**POR**-tant   French: *ang-**por-tah**ng*

See the difference?

PART 2. HOW TO PRONOUNCE FRENCH VOWELS

*F*or the newbie French learner, understanding the difference between **a, à,** and **â,** as well as **e, é, è,** and **ê,** can be head-swimmingly frustrating. However, the truth is it's not actually that complicated. Below is a nifty guide to help you easily distinguish between the pronunciation of each of the letters and their mind-boggling accents, or diacritical marks (those little *thingies* on top of the letters):

Vowels	Pronunciation Guide	Example	Wl the exa me
a	is pronounced like 'ah' in English	la	(the
à	is also pronounced like 'ah	là	(the
â	is pronounced like 'ah' but longer	âne	(do
e	When placed in the middle of a syllable, it is pronounced like ai in 'fair'	mer	(se;
e	When placed at the end of a syllable, it is pronounced like er in 'her'	le	(the
e	is silent at the end of a word	tasse	(cu
é	is pronounced like 'ay'	été	(su;
è	is pronounced like ai in 'fair'	père	(fat
ê	is also pronounced like ai in 'fair'	tête	(he;
i, y	are pronounced like ee in 'meet'	ski	(sk;
o	is pronounced like o in 'not'	poste	(po offi
ô	is pronounced like 'oh'	hôtel	(ho
u	this sound does not exist in English; say 'oo' with rounded lips	vu	(se(

Easy enough? Here is a quick recap on the vowel pronunciations:

- **a** and **à** are both pronounced 'ah' in English.

- **â** is also pronounced 'ah', except the sound is held longer.

- **e, è,** and **ê are** placed in the middle of a syllable, are pronounced 'ai' as in fair.

6

- The rule for pronouncing **e:** in the middle of a syllable, it is pronounced 'ai' as in *fair*; at the end of a syllable, it is pronounced 'er' as in *her*; at the end of a word, it is silent (e.g. *tasse*).

Now we will move on to the consonants.

PART 3. ALL ABOUT CONSONANTS

Consonants in French are basically pronounced the same as they are in English. Here is a quick guide to help you remember them:

Consonants	Pronunciation Guide	Example	What the example means
c	before e or i sounds like s	ceci	(this)
c	elsewhere it sounds like k	car	(coach)
ç	sounds like s	ça	(that)
ch	sounds like 'sh'	château	(castle)
g	before e or i sounds like s in 'measure'	général	(general)
g	elsewhere sounds like g in 'go'	gare	(station)
h	is silent	hôtel	(hotel)
j	sounds like s in 'measure'	je	(I)
qu, q	sound like k	qui	(who)
r	is pronounced at the back of the throat; it is quite similar to the sound we make when are gargling.	rire	(to laugh)
s	at the beginning of a word sounds like s	salle	(room)
s	between two vowels, it sounds like z	rose	(rose)

9

PART 3. ALL ABOUT CONSONANTS

Note: Except for the letters **c, f, l,** and **r**, consonants are not usually pronounced when they appear as the last letter of a word. For example, the **t** at the end of *passpor(t)* and the **s** at the end of *Pari(s)* are silent.

However, **c, f, l** and **r** are pronounced, such as in the words *hotel* and *professeur.*

To help you remember that these four consonants are exceptions, you can use this mnemonic device: **C**lear **F**rench **L**anguage **R**ecall or CFLR.

(See, told you this is easy!)

PART 4. WHAT ARE FRENCH NASAL SOUNDS?

*M*ost non-French speakers will usually describe the French language as having a "nasal" sound to it. These nasal sounds are quite distinctive of the French language and are characterized by the following:

1. They are produced by the blocking of air from leaving the mouth, causing it to be released through the nose.

2. These sounds are 'voiced,' which means the vocal cords vibrate to create the sound.

Sounds difficult? Not actually. In fact, the English language has three nasal sounds too, namely the 'm' sound, the 'n' sound, and the 'ng' sound. We are using these to speak flawlessly (or not!) everyday.

Try saying the words *sing, sang, song* and *sung* and you will notice the following: the letter **g** is given very little value in the standard pronunciation, and as you pronounce the words, air is blocked when the back of your tongue presses against the soft palate.

French has four nasal sounds that are more similar to their English counterparts than we realize. They are as follows:

PART 4. WHAT ARE FRENCH NASAL SOUNDS?

Nasal sound	Pronunciation	Example	What the Example Means
om, on	pronounce like ong in 'song'	nom non	(name) (no)
um*, un	pronounce like ung in 'sung'	un brun	(one) (brown)
am, an em, en	pronounce like 'ahng'	champ an temps en	(field) (year) (time) (in)
im*, in, aim, ain, ein	pronounce like ang in 'sang'	simple vin faim bain plein	(easy) (wine) (hunger) (bath) (full)
ien	pronounce like 'ee-ang'	bien	(well)

We mentioned that there are four nasal French sounds, so you may be wondering why there are five listed. This is because some French speakers do not make a distinction between **um*** and **im***, pronouncing both as 'ang' like we do in *sang*.

Syllable	Pronunciation	Example	What the Example Means
er	at the end of a word of two syllables or more sounds like 'ay'	parler	(to speak)
ez	at the end of a word sounds like 'ay'	nez	(nose)
ail	at the end of a word sounds like 'ah'ee'	travail	(work)
eil, eille	sound like 'a'ee'	soleil bouteille	(sun) (bouteille)
ill	usually sounds like 'ee'y'	billet	(ticket)
gn	sounds like ni in 'onion'	signal	(signal

PART 5. ALL THE FRENCH-Y VARIATIONS

*N*ow read carefully because this is where non-French speakers often get into trouble. Listed below are some pronunciations for syllables that, when spoken, differ quite a bit from how they are pronounced in English:

> **Er** (when at the end of a word with two or more syllables) and **ez** are both pronounced like 'ay'. As an exception to the **c, f, l, r** consonants pronunciation rule presented earlier, **l,** when used in the syllables **ail** and **eil**, is generally silent. Surely you are quite familiar with the 'gn' sound already (especially if you are the lasa**gn**a-eating type!).

PART 6. THOSE FLOWING, CONNECTED SOUNDS AND HOW IT IS DONE

We are all quite aware that the French language has a flowing and uninterrupted quality to its sound, or, to put it jokingly, sounds like one is speaking in cursive. This lends the language a lot of charm and a very noticeable melodic sound that foreigners simply love.

To achieve this delightfully melodious sound in intonation, here is a simple rule for you to remember:

If a word that begins with a vowel or a silent **h** follows a word that ends in a consonant, the consonant is linked to the beginning of the second word.

Simply stated, IF:

1st word — ends in a consonant

2nd word — begins with a vowel or silent H

Result: the consonant at the end of the first word is automatically linked to the beginning vowel of the second word.

PART 6. THOSE FLOWING, CONNECTED ....

To illustrate this concept, here are a few examples:

1. *nous avons* – the 1st word (nous) ends with a consonant, while the 2nd word (avons) begins with a vowel.

   Pronunciation: noo **zah**-vong (meaning 'we have')

2. 2. un petit enfant – the 1st word (petit) ends with a consonant, while the 2nd word (enfant) begins with a vowel.

   Pronunciation: ung p'tee **tahng**-fahng (meaning 'a small child')

Here are a few guidelines to remember when using other letter combinations:

Letters	Sound	Example	Pronunciation	What the example means
s, x	sounds like z	deux ans	der zahng	two years
d	sounds like t	un grand arbre	ung grahng tahbr	a tall tree
f	sounds like v	neuf heures	ner verr	nine hours

18

PART 7. ACCENT MARKS (AND THE DIFFERENCE THEY MAKE)

*J*ust like several other languages, the French language makes use of accent marks. Accents are a type of diacritic mark, which is basically a glyph, or a small sign attached to a letter. These are commonly used in Latin-derived alphabets as well as non-Latin ones like Chinese, Arabic, Greek, Hebrew, and Korean.

French makes use of three main accents:

- The acute accent **(é)** or *l'accent aigu,* which can be found in the letter **e**

- The grave accent **(è)** or *l'accent grave,* which can be found in the letters **a, e,** and **u**

- The circumflex **(ê)** or *l'accent circonflexe* which can be found in any vowel

In addition, there is the cedilla (**ç**) or *la cedilla,* which can be found only underneath the letter **c,** and the diaeresis (**ë**) or *le tréma,* which is often used to indicate that the second vowel is to be pronounced separately from the first (e.g. naïf, which means *naïve,* and noel, which means *Christmas*).

"So, what are accent marks for?" you might ask. Here are their uses:

First, they are used to change how a letter sounds. Let's take for example the letter **e**. The unaccented **e** sounds like 'er' in *her* The **é** acute sounds like 'ay' in *say* The **è** grave sounds like 'ai' in *fair*.

For the cedilla, remember the rule discussed earlier wherein **c** is only pronounced as a soft **s** when placed before an **e** or **i**? The cedilla totally changes that. Take for example the word *garçon* (which means boy). It precedes an **o**, which means it should be pronounced as a hard **c** as in *car*, but the cedilla softens the letter to make it sound like an **s** as in *sit*.

Second, accent marks are used to differentiate between similarly spelled words that have different meanings.

Examples:

- **la** (the) versus **là** (there)

- **ou** (or) versus. **où** (where)

- **sur** (on) versus **sûr** (sure)

There is something very interesting about the accents, however. In modern usage, French accents usually do not appear in capital letters because it is deemed unnecessary. The Académie Française, however, maintains that accents should be used at all times in order to avoid confusion.

PART 8. FRENCH AND ENGLISH SIMILARITIES

*C*ontrary to popular belief, there is not a significant difference between English and French pronunciation. In fact, most syllables are pronounced as though they are part of an English word and are each given equal stress.

However, take note of the following rule while reading the examples shown in this guide:

- *ng* (italics)   must never be pronounced; these letters merely indicate that the preceding vowel has a nasal sound.

- e*r* (r italics)   do not pronounce the r; this syllable sounds like er in 'her'.

- zh   sounds like s in 'measure'.

- ü   no equivalent in English; round your lips and say 'ee'.

- o   sounds like o in 'not'.

- oh   sounds like o in 'note'.

PART 9. THE FRENCH ALPHABET

*T*he French Alphabet also contains 26 letters of the ISO basic Latin-script alphabet (or, simply, the alphabet as we know it). It is similar to that of the English alphabet except for **K** and **W,** which are not always used. The pronunciation is also a bit different. So, just in case you are planning to visit France soon, you might want to practice spelling your name out phonetically should the French-speaking receptionist (or other people essential to your travel) require it. Spelling it out in French would make a lot more sense to them than using the English phonetics.

Here is an example:

If your name is JANEY, it is spelled out as *'zheel – ah – en – er – ee-grek'.*

Here is the rest of the French alphabet as well as the letters' pronunciations:

PART 9. THE FRENCH ALPHABET

A (ah)	B (bay)	C (say)	D (day)	E (er)
F (ef)	G (zhay)	H (ahsh)	I (ee)	J (zheel)
K (kah)	L (el)	M (em)	N (en)	O (oh)
P (pay)	Q (kü)	R(airr)	S (ess)	T (tay)
U (ü)	V (vay)	W (doobl-vay)	X (eeks)	Y (ee-grek)
Z (zed)				

Try to practice saying these pronunciations as often as you can, as this will help you advance in your learning. Remember, just like any other skill, all it takes is determination and consistency for you to develop the habit. Exposing yourself to the French language in movies, videos, and even audio books can help you become more familiar with the words and sounds, making it easier to learn them.

Part 1: Essentials / L'essentiel

Chapter 1: The basics / La base

*T*his chapter will be the most useful when you need help getting out of a difficult situation.

Bonjour / Salut (inf)
Hello / Hi
boñ-zhoor/sa-lew

Au revoir/Salut
Goodbye/Bye
oh ruh-vwar/sa-lew

Pardon, monsieur/madame!
Excuse me! (to catch attention)
par-doñ, muh-syuh/ma-dam!

Pardon!
Sorry!
par-doñ!

Je suis désolé(e)
I'm sorry
zhuh swee day-zo-lay

Merci (beaucoup)
Thanks (very much)
mehr-see {boh-koo)

S'il vous plaît
Please
seel voo pleh

Parlez-vous anglais?
Do you speak English?
par-lay-voo ahn-gleh?

Y a-t-il quelqu'un ici qui parle anglais?
Does anyone here speak English?
Ya a-tteel kel-kuhn eesee kee par long-gley?

Je ne parle que l'anglais
I speak only English
zhuh nuh parl kuh long-gley

Je parle un peu français
I speak a little French
Zhuh parl uhn puh frahn-seh

Veuillez parler plus lentement
Please speak more slowly
vuh-yay par-lay plew lahnt-mahn

Je (ne) comprends (pas)
I (do not) understand
zhuh (nuh) kawn-prahn (pah)

Me comprenez-vous?
Do you understand me?
muh kawn-pruh-nay-voo?

Veuillez répéter, s'il vous plaît
Repeat It, please
vuh-yay ray-pay-tay, seel voo pleh

Écrivez-le, s›il vous plaît
Write it down, please
ay-kree-vay-luh, seel voo pleh

Que veut dire ceci?
What does this mean?
kuh vuh deer suh-see?

De rien
You are welcome
duh ree-en

Comment dit-on «xx» en français?
How do you say "xx" in French?
kaw-mahn dee-tawn "x" ehn frahn-seh?

Comment épelez-vous "xx"?
How do you spell "xx"?
kaw-mahn tay-play-voo "x"?

Qu'est-ce que c'est que ça?
What is that?
kes-kuh seh kuh sa?

Non
No
nawn

Part 1: Essentials / L'essentiel

Pardon
Excuse me
par-down

Peut-être
Perhaps
puh-TEH-truh

Oui
Yes
wee

Je suis Américain
I am a United States citizen
zhuh swee za-may-ree-kang

Mon adresse (pour le courrier) est XX
My (mailing) address is XX
maw na-dress {poor luh koor-yay) eh XX

Que désirez-vous?
What do you wish?
kuh Day-zee-ray-voo?

Venez ici
Come here
vuh-nay zee-see

Entrez
Come in
ahn-tray

Attendez un moment
Wait a moment
at-tahn-day zûhn mo-mahn

Je suis pressé
I am in a hurry
zhuh swee pres-say

J'ai chaud, froid
I am warm, cold
zhay shoh, frwah

J'ai faim, soif
I am hungry, thirsty
zhay fen, swahf

Je suis occupé, fatigué
I am busy, tired
zhuh swee zaw-kew-pay, fa-tee-gay

Je suis content
I am glad
zhahn swee kawn-tahn

Je regrette
I am sorry
zhuh ruh-gret

Qu'y a-t-il?
What is the matter here?
kee a-teel?

Part 1: Essentials / L'essentiel

C'est bien
It is all right
seh byen

Je (ne) sais (pas)
I (do not) know
zhuh (nuh) say (pah)

Je (ne) le crois (pas)
I (do not) think so
zhuh (nuh) luh krwah (pah)

Ça ne fait rien
It doesn't matter
sa nuh feh ree-en

Combien est-ce?
How much is it?
kaum-byen ess?

C'est tout
That is all
seh too

Pouvez-vous m'aider (me dire)?
Can you help me (tell me)?
poo-veah-voo may-day (muh deer)?

Où sont les lavabos?
Where is the washroom?
oo sawn lay la-va-boh?

Les toilettes pour hommes
The men's room
Lay twa·let poor om

Les toilettes pour femmes
The ladies room
Lay twa·let poor fam

Je cherche mon hôtel
I am looking for my hôtel
zhuh shehrsh maw no-tel

Je voudrais y aller à pied
I would like to walk there
zhuh voo-dreh zee al-lay ah pyay

Pourquoi?
Why?
poor-kwah?

Quand?
When?
kahn?

Qui?
Who?
kee?

Quoi?
What?
kwah?

31

Comment?
How?
kaw-mahn?

Combien de temps?
How long?
kawn-byen duh tahn?

À quelle distance?
How far?
ah kel deess-tahns?

Ici
Here
ee-see

Là
There
lah

À
To
ah

De
From
duh

Avec
With
a-vek

Sans
Without
sahn

Dans
In
dahn

Sur
on
sewr

Près de
Near
preh duh

Loin de
Far
lwen duh

Devant
In front of
duh-vahm

Derrière
Behind
day-ryehr

À côté de
Beside
ah koh-tay duh

À l'intérieur
Inside
ah len-tay-ryuhr

À l'extérieur
Outside
ah lex-tay-ryuhr

Vide
Empty
veed

Plein
Full
pluhn

Quelque chose
Something
kel-kuh shohz

Rien
Nothing
ree-en

Plusieurs
Several
plewzyuhr

Quelques
Few
kel-kuh

(Beaucoup) plus
(Much) more
(boh-koo) plewss

Moins
Less
mwen

(Un peu) plus
(A little) more
(uhn puh) plewss

Assez
Enough
as-say

Trop
Too much
troh

Beaucoup
Many
boh-koo

Bon
Good
bawn

Meilleur (que)
Better (than)
may-yuhr (kuh)

Le meilleur
The Best
luh may-yuhr

Mauvais
Bad
moh-vay

Pire (que)
Worse (than)
peer (kuh)

Maintenant
Now
ment-nahn

Tout de suite
Immediately
toot sweet

Bientôt
Soon
byen-toh

Plus tard
Later
plew tahr

Le plus tôt possible
As soon as possible
luh plew toh paw-SEE- bluh

Il est (trop) tard
It is (too) late
eeleh (troh) tahr

Il est tôt
It is early
eel eh toh

Lentement
Slowly
lanhtuh-mahn

Plus lentement
Slower
plew lahntuh-mahn

Vite
Quickly
veet

Plus vite
Faster
plew veet

Attention!
Look on!
ah-tahn-syawn

Écoutez
Listen
ay-koo-tay

Regardez
Look here
ruh-gar-day

Comprenez-vous?
Do you understand?
kom·pre·ney·voo

Que veut dire (XX)?
What does (XX) mean?
ke veu deer (XX)

Comment …?
How do you …?
ko·mon …

le prononcez-vous
pronounce this
le pro·non·sey voo

est-ce qu'on écrit (bonjour)
write (bonjour)
es kon ey·kree (bon·zhoor)

38

Chapter 2 : Difficulties / Difficultés

Je ne peux pas trouver l'adresse de mon hôtel
I cannot find my hotel address
zhuh nuh puh pah troo-vay la-dress duh maw no-ttel

J'ai perdu mes amis
I have lost my friends
zhay pehr-dew may za-mee

J'ai laissé mon sac, mon portefeuille à l'hôtel
I left my purse, wallet in the hotel
zhay lay-say mawn sahk, mawn pawrt-Foo-yuh ah lo-tel

J'ai oublié mon argent, mes clés
I forgot my money, keys
zhay oo-blee-ay maw nar-zhahn, may klay

J'ai manqué mon train
I have missed my train
zhay mahn-kay mawn tren

Que dois-je faire?
What am I to do?
kuh DWAH-zhuh fehr?

Mes lunettes sont cassées
My glasses are broken
may lew-net sawn kas-say

Où peut-on les faire réparer?
Where can they be repaired?
oo puh-tawn lay fehr ray-pa-ray?

Un appareil acoustique
A hearing aid
uh nap-pa-ray a-kooss teek

Le bureau des objets trouvés
The lost and found desk
luh bew-roh day zawb-zheh troo-vay

Le consulat des États-Unis
The American consulate
luh kawn-sew-la day zay-ta-zew-nee

Le commissariat de police
The police station
luh kaw-mee-sa-rya duh paw-leess

Je vais appeler un agent
I will call a policeman
zhuh vay za-play uh na-zhahn

on m'a volé.
I've been robbed.
on ma vo·ley

J'ai perdu ...
I've lost my ...
zhey pair·dew ...

on m'a volé …
… was/were stolen.
on ma vo·ley …

mon sac à dos
my backpack
mon sak a do

mes valises
my bags
mey va·leez

ma carte de crédit
my credit card
ma kart de krey·dee

mon sac à main
my handbag
mon sak a mun

mes bijoux
my jewellery
mey bee·zhoo

mon argent
my money
mon ar zhon

mon passeport
my passport
mom pas·por

mes chèques de voyage
my travellers cheques
mey shek de vwa·yazh

mon portefeuille
my wallet
mom por·te·feu·ye

Je veux contacter mon …
I want to contact my …
zhuh veu kon·tak·tey mon …

consulat
consulate
kon·sew·la

ambassade
embassy
om·ba·sad

Part 2: Talking to people / Parler aux gens

Chapter 3 : Interraction / Intéraction

*T*he main point of speaking French is to use the language in everyday conversation. As intimidating as it can be to converse in a different language, this is the ultimate goal of your studies. It is a good idea to have some basic phrases up your sleeve for when you are having conversations with people in French. These handy conversation starters and tips are ideal for those times when you need something relevant to say to keep the dialogue going.

S'il vous plaît
Please
seel voo pleh

Merci (beaucoup)
Thanks (very much)
mehr-see (boh-koo)

De rien!
You're welcome!
duh ryañ!

Oui
Yes
Wee

Non
No
Noñ

Oui, merci
Yes, please
wee, mehr-see

Non, merci
No, thanks
noñ, mehr-see

D'accord!
OK!
da-kor!

Monsieur/M.
Sir/Mr
muh-syuh

Madame/Mme
Madam/Mrs/Ms
ma-dam

Mademoiselle/Mlle
Miss
mad-mwa-zel

Bonjour/Salut
Hello/Hi
boñ-zhoor/sa-lew

44

Au revoir/Salut
Goodbye/Bye
oh ruh-vwar/sa-lew

À bientôt
Bye for now
a byañ-toh

Bonsoir
Good evening
boñ-swar

Bonne nuit
Goodnight
bon nwee

À demain
See you tomorrow
a duh-mañ

Pardon, monsieur/madame!
Excuse me! (to catch attention)
par-doñ, muh-syuh/ma-dam!

Pardon!
Sorry!
par-doñ!

Je suis désolé(e)
I'm sorry
zhuh swee day-zo-lay

Part 2: Talking to people / Parler aux gens

Comment allez-vous?
How are you?
ko-mahñ ta-lay voo?

Très bien, merci
Fine, thanks
treh byañ, mehr-see

Et vous?
And you?
ay voo?

Je ne comprends pas
I don't understand
zhuh nuh koñ-prahñ pa

Je parle très peu le français
I speak very little French
zhuh parl treh puh luh frahñ-seh

Est-ce que je peux…?
Can I…?
es kuh zhuh puh…?

fumer
Smoke
few-may

Qu'est-ce que ça veut dire?
What does this mean?
kes kuh sa vuh deer?

Le repas était délicieux
The meal was delicious
luh ruh-pa ay-teh day-lee-syuh

Je vous remercie
Thank you very much
zhuh voo ruh-mehr-see

Enchanté(e)
Delighted to meet you
ahñ-shahñ-tay

Voici...
This is...
vwa-see...

mon mari/ma femme
my husband/my wife
moñ ma-ree/ma fam

Passez de bonnes vacances!
Enjoy your holiday!
pa-say duh bon va-kahñs!

Quel est votre ...? Quel est ton ...? Inf
What's your ...?
kel ey vo·tre ... kel ey ton ...

adresse
address
a·dress

e-mail
email address
ey·mel

numéro de fax
fax number
new·mey·ro de faks

numéro de téléphone
phone number
new·mey·ro de tehlehfohn

Vous faites quoi comme métier? pol
What's your occupation?
voo fet kwa kom mey·tyey

Tu fais quoi comme métier? inf
What's your occupation?
tew fey kwa kom mey·tyey

Je suis un/une … m/f
I'm a/an …
zhe swee zun/zewn …

Vous venez d'où? pol
Where are you from?
voo ve·ney doo

Tu viens d'où? inf
Where are you from?
tew vyun doo

Je viens …
I'm from …
zhe vyun …

d'Australie
Australia
dos·tra·lee

du Canada
Canada
dew ka·na·da

d'Angleterre
England
dong·gle·tair

de la Nouvelle-Zélande
New Zealand
de la noo·vel·zey·lond

des USA
the USA
dey zew·es·a

Est-ce que vous êtes marié(e)? m/f pol
Are you married?
es·ke voo zet mar·yey

Est-ce que tu es marié(e)? m/f inf
Are you married?
es·ke tew ey mar·yey

Je suis marié/mariée. m/f
I'm married.
zhe swee mar·yey

Je suis célibataire. m&f
I'm single.
zhe swee sey·lee·ba·tair

Quel âge ...?
How old ...?
kel azh ...

avez-vous pol
are you
a·vey·voo

As-tu ...? Inf
are you
a·tew

a votre fille pol
is your daughter
a vo·tre fee·ye

a votre fils pol
is your son
a vo·tre fees

J'ai ... ans.
I'm ... years old
zhey ... on

Il/Elle a … ans.
He/She is … years old.
eel/el a … on

Je (ne) suis (pas)…
I'm (not) …
zhe (ne) swee (pa) …

Êtes-vous …? pol
Are you …?
et voo …

Es·tu …
Are you …?
Ey-tew …? inf

petit ami
boyfriend
pe-tee ta-mee

frère
brother
frair

fille
daughter
fee-ye

père
father
pair

ami/amie m/f
friend
a-mee

petite amie
girlfriend
pe-teet a-mee

mari
husband
ma-ree

mère
mother
mair

partenaire
partner
par-te-nair

sœur
sister
seur

fils
son
fees

femme
wife
fam

Voici mon …
Here's my …
vwa-see mon …

Mon frère
My brother
mawn frehr

Mon ami
My friend
maw na-mee

Ma femme
My wife
mafahm

Mon mari
My husband
mawn ma-ree

Ma sœur
My sister
ma suhr

Ma fille
My daughter
ma fee-yuh

Mon fils
My son
mawn fees

Mon enfant
My child
maw nahn-fahn

Le garçon
The boy
luh gar-sawn

La jeune fille
The girl
la zhuhn FEE-yuh

L'homme
The man
lawm

La femme
The woman
lafahm

heureux/heureuse m/f
happy
er-reu/er-reuz

triste m&f
sad
treest

froid/froide m/f
cold
frwa/frwad

chaud/chaude m/f
hot
sho/shod

faim m&f
hungry
fum

soif m&f
thirsty
swaf

Parlez-vous anglais?
Do you speak English?
par-lay-voo ong-gley?

Y a-t-il quelqu'un ici qui parle anglais?
Does anyone here speak English?
Ya a-ttel kel kuhn eesee kee par ong-gley?

Je ne parle que l'anglais
I speak only English
zhuh nuh parl kuh long-gley

Je parle un peu français
I speak a little French
Zhuh parl ahn puh frahn-seh

Veuillez parler plus lentement
Please speak more slowly
vuh-yay par-lay plew lahnt-mahn

Me comprenez-vous?
Do you understand me?
muh kawn-pruh-nay-voo?

Veuillez répéter, s'il vous plaît
Repeat It, please
vuh-yay ray-pay-tay, seel voo pleh

Écrivez-le, s›il vous plaît
Write it down, please
ay-kree-vay-luh, seel ooo pleh

Que veut dire ceci?
What does this mean?
kuh vuh deer suh-see?

De rien
You are welcome
duh ree-en

Comment dit-on «xx» en français?
How do you say "xx" in French?
kaw-mahn dee-tawn "xx" ahn frahn-seh?

Comment épelez-vous "xx"?
How do you spell "xx"?
kaw-mahn tay-play-voo "x"?

Qu'est-ce que c'est que ça?
What is that?
kes-kuh seh kuh sa?

Peut-être
Perhaps
puh-TEH-truh

Je suis Américain
I am a United States citizen
zhuh swee za-may-ree-kang

Mon adresse (pour le courrier) est XX
My (mailing) address is XX
maw na-dress {poor luh koor-yay) eh XX

Que désirez-vous?
What do you wish?
kuh day-zee-ray-voo?

Venez ici
Come here
vuh-nay zee-see

Entrez
Come in
ahn-tray

Attendez un moment
Wait a moment
at-tahn-day zûhn mo-mahn

Je suis pressé
I am in a hurry
zhuh swee pres-say

J'ai chaud, froid
I am warm, cold
zhay shoh,frwah

J'ai faim, soif
I am hungry, thirsty
zhay fen, swahf

Je suis occupé, fatigué
I am busy, tired
zhuh swee zaw-kew-pa, fa-tee-gay

J'en suis content
I am glad
zhahn swee kawn-tahn

Je regrette
I am sorry
zhuh ruh-gret

Qu'y a-t-il?
What is the matter here?
kee ya-teel?

C'est bien
It is all right
seh byen

Je (ne) sais (pas)
I (do not) know
zhuh (nuh) say (pah)

Je (ne) le crois (pas)
I (do not) think so
(zhuh nuh) luh krwah (pah)

Ça ne fait rien
It doesn't matter
sa nuh feh ree-en

Combien est-ce?
How much is it?
kaum-byen ess?

C'est tout
That is all
seh too

Pouvez-vous m'aider (me dire)?
Can you help me (tell me)?
poo-vay-voo may-day (muh deer)?

Où sont les lavabos?
Where is the washroom?
oo sawn lay la-va-boh?

Pour Messieurs
The men's room
Poor may-syuh

Pour Dames
The ladies room
Poor dahm

Je cherche mon hôtel
I am looking for my hotel
zhuh shehrsh maw no-tel

Je voudrais y aller à pied
I would like to walk there
zhuh wo-dreh zee al-lay ah pyay

Pourquoi?
Why?
poor-kwah?

Quand?
When?
kahn?

Qui?
Who?
kee?

Quoi?
What?
kwah?

Comment?
How?
kaw-mahn?

Combien de temps?
How long?
kawn-byen duh tahn?

À quelle distance?
How far?
ah kel deess-tahns?

Ici
Here
ee-see

Là
There
la

À
To
ah

De
From
duh

Avec
With
a-vek

Sans
Without
sahn

Dans
In
dahn

Sur
on
Suhr

Près de
Near
preh duh

Loin de
Far
lwen duh

Devant
In front of
duh-vahm

Derrière
Behind
day-ryehr

À côté de
Beside
ah koh-tay duh

À l'intérieur
Inside
ah len-tay-ryuhr

À l'extérieur
Outside
ah lex-tay-ryuhr

Vide
Empty
veed

Plein
Full
plun

Quelque chose
Something
kel-kuh-shohz

Rien
Nothing
ree-en

Plusieurs
Several
plewzyuhr

Quelques
Few
kel-kuh

(Beaucoup) plus
(Much) more
(boh-koo) plewss

Moins
Less
mwen

(Un peu) plus
(A little) more
(uhn puh) plewss

Assez
Enough
as-say

Trop
Too much
troh

Beaucoup
Many
boh-koo

Bon
Good
bawn

Meilleur (que)
Better (than)
may-yuhr (kuh)

Le meilleur
The best
luh may-yuhr

Mauvais
Bad
moh-veh

Pire (que)
Worse (than)
peer (kuh)

Maintenant
Now
ment-nah~n

Tout de suite
Immediately
toot sweet

Bientôt
Soon
byen-toh

Plus tard
Later
plew tahr

Le plus tôt possible
As soon as possible
luh plew toh paw-SEE- bluh

Il est (trop) tard
It is (too) late
eeleh (troh) tahr

Il est tôt
It is early
eel eh toh

Lentement
Slowly
lahnt-mahn

Plus lentement
Slower
plew lahnt-mahn

Vite
Quickly
veet

Plus vite
Faster
plew veet

Attention!
Look on!
ah-tahn-syawn

Écoutez
Listen
ay-koo-tay

Regardez
Look here
ruh-gar-day

Parlez-vous anglais?
Do you speak English?
par-ley-voo ong-gley

Que veut dire (beaucoup)?
What does (beaucoup) mean?
ke veu deer (bo-koo)

Comment …?
How do you …?
ko-mon …

le prononcez-vous
pronounce this
le pro-non-sey voo

est-ce qu'on écrit (bonjour)
write (bonjour)
es kon ey-kree (bon-zhoor)

Pourriez-vous … ?
Could you…
poo-ree-yey voo …

s'il vous plaît?
please …?
seel voo pley

répéter
repeat that
rey-pey-tey

parler plus lentement
speak more slowly
par-ley plew lon-te-mon

l'écrire
write it down
ley-kreer

Je vous souhaite un/une…
I'd like to wish you a…
zhuh voo soo-eht uñ/ewn…

Bonne Année!
Happy New Year!
bon a-nay!

Joyeuses Pâques!
Happy Easter!
zhwa-yuz pak!

Bon anniversaire!
Happy birthday!
boñ na-nee-vehr-sehr!

Bon voyage!
Have a good trip!
boñ vwa-yazh!

Bon appétit!
Enjoy your meal!
boñ na-pay-tee!

Comment tu t'appelles?
What's your name?
ko-mahñ tew ta-pel?

Je m'appelle…
My name is…
zhuh ma-pel…

Tu es d'où?
Where are you from?
tew ay doo?

Je suis anglais(e), de Londres
I am English, from London
zhuh swee zahñ-gleh(z), duh loñdr

Enchanté(e)!
Pleased to meet you!
on-shon-tay

Chapter 4 Get to know somebody - Faire connaissance

Quel âge as-tu?
How old are you?
kel azh a tew?

J'ai ... ans
I'm ... years old
zhay ... ahñ

Tu es français(e)?
Are you French?
tew ay frahñ-seh(z)?

Je suis anglais(e)/ écossais(e)/américain(e)
I'm English/Scottish/American
zhuh swee zong-gley (z)/zay-*koseh(z)/za-mayree-kañ/ken*

Où est-ce que tu habites?
Where do you live?
oo es kuh tew a-beet?

Où est-ce que vous habitez?
Where do you live? (plural)
oo es kuh voo za-bee-tay?

J'habite à Londres
I live in London
zha-beet a loñdr

Nous habitons à Glasgow
We live in Glasgow
noo za-bee-toñ a glaz-goh

Je suis...
I'm...
zhuh swee...

célibataire
single
say-lee-ba-tehr

marié(e)
married
mar-yay

divorcé(e)
divorced
dee-vor-say

J'ai...
I have...
zhay...

un petit ami
a boyfriend
uñ puh-tee-ta-mee

une petite amie
a girlfriend
ewn puh-teet a-mee

71

Part 2: Talking to people / Parler aux gens

J'ai un compagnon/une compagne
I have a partner (male/female)
zhay uñ kom-pa-nyoñ/ewn koñ-panyuh

J'ai ... enfants
I have ... children
zhay ... ahñ-fahñ

Je n'ai pas d'enfants
I have no children
zhuh nay pas dahñ-fahñ

Je suis ici en vacances/ en voyage d'affaires/ en week-end
I'm here on holiday/on business/for the weekend
zhuh swee zee-see ahñ va-kahñs/ahñ vwa-yazh da-fehr/ahñ wee-kend

Qu'est-ce que vous faites comme travail?
What work do you do?
kes kuh voo fet kom tra-va-yuh?

Je suis...
I'm...
zhuh swee...

médecin
a doctor
may-dsañ

directeur
a manager
dee-rek-tur

secrétaire
a secretary
suh-kray-tehr

Je travaille à domicile
I work from home
zhuh tra-va-yuh a do-mee-seel

Je travaille à mon compte
I'm self-employed
zhuh tra-va-yuh a moñ koñt

Part 3 : Directions, Transport, Etc / La direction, les transports...

*T*here is nothing worse than feeling lost, let alone being lost in a foreign country. Learning French has, of course, some very practical uses when you are in a French speaking country. When travelling, having a basic understanding of how to ask for directions or simply knowing the words for public transportation can make all the difference in your experience.

Chapter 5 Asking the way / Demander la direction

en face de
opposite of
ahñ fas duh

à côté de
next to
a ko-tay duh

près de
near to
preh duh

le carrefour
crossroad
luh kar-foor

le rond-point
roundabout
luh roñ-pwañ

Pardon, pour aller à la gare?
Excuse me, how do I get to the station?
par-doñ, poor a-lay a la gar?

Continuez tout droit, après l'église tournez à gauche/à droite
Keep straight on, after the church turn left/right
koñ-tee-new-ay too drwa, a-preh lay-gleez toor-nay a gohsh/a drwat

C'est loin?
Is it far?
say lwañ?

Non, c'est à deux cents mètres/à cinq minutes
No, 200 yards/five minutes
noñ, say ta duh sahñ metr/a sañk mee-newt

Merci!
Thank you!
mehr-see!

Nous cherchons...
We're looking for...
noo shehr-shoñ...

On peut y aller à pied?
Can we walk there?
oñ puh ee a-lay a pyay?

Nous nous sommes perdu(e)s
We're lost
noo noo som pehr-dew

C'est la bonne direction pour...?
Is this the right way to...?
say la bon dee-rek-syoñ poor...?

Pouvez-vous me montrer sur la carte?
Can you show me on the map?
poo-vay voo me moñ-tray sewr la kart?

C'est indiqué
It's signposted
say tañ-dee-kay

C'est au coin de la rue
It's on the corner of the street
say toh kwañ duh la rew

C'est là-bas
It's over there
say la-ba

Chapter 6 Bus and coach / Le bus

Pardon, quel bus pour le centre-ville?
Excuse me, which bus goes to the centre?
par-doñ, kel bews poor luh sahñtr veel?

Le 10
Number 10
luh deess

Où est l'arrêt?
Where is the bus stop?
oo ay la-reh?

Là-bas, à gauche
There, on the left
la-ba, a gohsh

Où est-ce que je peux acheter des tickets de bus?
Where can I buy bus tickets?
oo es kuh zhuh puh ash-tay day tee-keh duh bews?

Là-bas, au distributeur
Over there, at the ticket machine
la-ba, oh dees-tree-bew-tur

Est-ce qu'il y a un bus pour...?
Is there a bus to...?
es keel ya uñ bews poor...?

Où est-ce qu'on prend le bus pour aller à/au (etc.)…?
Where do I catch the bus to go to…?
oo es koñ prahñ luh bews poor a-lay a/oh…?

C'est combien pour aller à/au (etc.)…?
How much is it to…?
say koñ-byañ poor a-lay a/oh…?

au centre
to the centre
oh sahñtr

à la plage
to the beach
a la plazh

aux magasins
to the shops
oh ma-ga-zañ

à Montmartre
to Montmartre
a moñ-martr

Les bus pour … passent tous les combien?
How frequent are the buses to…?
lay bews poor … pas too lay koñ-byañ?

À quelle heure part le premier/le dernier bus pour…?
When is the first/the last bus to…?
a kel ur par luh pruh-myay/ luh dehr-nyay bews poor…?

Pourriez-vous me dire quand descendre?
Could you tell me when to get off?
poo-ree-ay-voo muh deer kahñ deh-sahñdr?

C'est mon arrêt
This is my stop
say moñ na-reh

Prenez le métro, c'est plus rapide
Take the metro, it's quicker
pruh-nay luh may-troh, say plew ra-peed

Chapter 7 Metro / Le métro

entrée
entrance
ahñ-tray

sortie
way out/exit
sor-tee

la ligne de métro
metro line
la lee-nyuh duh may-troh

en direction de...
in the direction of...
ahñ dee-rek-syoñ duh...

correspondence
connecting line
ko-reh-spoñ-dahñs

Où est la station de métro la plus proche?
Where is the nearest metro?
oo ay la sta-syoñ duh may-troh la plew prosh?

Je vais à...
I'm going to...
zhuh veh a...

Comment marche le guichet automatique?
How does the ticket machine work?
ko-mahñ marsh luh gee-sheh oh-toh-ma-teek?

Vous avez un plan du métro?
Do you have a map of the metro?
voo za-vay uñ plahñ dew may-troh?

Pour aller à/au (etc.)…?
How do I get to…?
poor a-lay a/oh…?

Est-ce qu'il faut changer?
Do I have to change?
es keel foh shañ-zhay?

C'est quelle ligne pour…?
Which line is it for…?
say kel lee-nyuh poor…?

Dans quelle direction?
In which direction?
dahñ kel dee-rek-syoñ?

Quel est le prochain arrêt?
What is the next stop?
kel ay luh pro-shañ na-reh?

Chapter 8 Train – Le train

horaire
timetable
o-rehr

circuler
to operate
seer-kew-lay

dimanches et fêtes
Sundays and holidays
dee-mahñsh ay fet

accès aux quais
access to the platforms
ak-seh oh keh

Quand part le prochain train pour…?
When is the next train to…?
kahñ par luh pro-shañ trañ poor…?

A 17 heures 10
At ten past five
a dee-set ur dees

Deux billets pour…
Two tickets to…
duh bee-yeh poor…

Aller simple ou aller-retour?
Single or return?
a-lay sañpl oo a-lay-ruh-toor?

Première classe/Deuxième classe
First class/Second class
pruh myehr klas/duh-zyem klas

Fumeur/Non fumeur
Smoking/Non-smoking
few-mur/noñ few-mur

Y a-t-il un supplément à payer?
Is there a supplement to pay?
ee a-teel uñ sew-play-mahñ a payyay?

Je voudrais réserver une place dans le TGV pour Nîmes
I want to book a seat on the TGV to Nîmes
zhuh voo-dreh ray-zehr-vay ewn plas dahñ luh tay-zhay-vay poor neem

Le train pour ... est à quelle heure?
When is the train to...?
luh trañ poor ... ay ta kel ur?

le premier/le dernier
the first/the last
luh pruh myay/luh dehr-nyay

À quelle heure arrive-t-il à...?
When does it arrive in...?
a kel ur a-reev-teel a...?

Est-ce qu'il faut changer?
Do I have to change?
es keel foh shañ-zhay?

Il part de quel quai?
Which platform does it leave from?
eel par duh kel kay?

C'est le bon quai pour le train de Paris?
Is this the right platform for the train to Paris?
say luh boñ kay poor luh trañ duh pa-ree?

C'est le train pour...?
Is this the train for...?
say luh trañ poor...?

Il part à quelle heure?
When does it leave?
eel par a kel ur?

Est-ce que le train s'arrête à...?
Does the train stop at...?
es kuh luh trañ sa-ret a...?

Où dois-je changer pour...?
Where do I change for...?
oo dwa-zhuh shahñ-zhay poor...?

S'il vous plaît, prévenez-moi quand nous serons à...
Please tell me when we get to...
seel voo pleh, pray-vnay mwa kañ noo suh-roñ za...

Cette place est-elle libre?
Is this seat free?
set plas ay-tel leebr?

Excusez-moi
Excuse me
eks-kew-zay-mwa

Pardon!
Sorry!
par-doñ!

Chapter 9 Taxi – Le taxi

la station de taxis
taxi rank
la sta-syoñ duh tak-see

Je voudrais un taxi
I want a taxi
zhuh voo-dreh uñ tak-see

Où est-ce que je peux prendre un taxi?
Where can I get a taxi?
oo es kuh zhuh puh prahñdr uñ tak-see?

Pouvez-vous m'appeler un taxi?
Could you order me a taxi?
poo-vay voo ma-play uñ tak-see?

Combien ça va coûter pour aller à/au (etc.)...?
How much is it going to cost to go to...?
koñ-byañ sa va koo-tay poor a-lay a/oh...?

au centre-ville
to the town centre
oh sahñtr-veel

à la gare
to the station
a la gar

à l'aéroport
to the airport
a la-ay-ro-por

à cette adresse
to this address
a set a-dres

C'est combien?
How much is it?
say koñ-byañ?

C'est plus qu'au compteur
It's more than on the meter
say plew skoh koñ-tur

Gardez la monnaie
Keep the change
gar-day la mo-neh

Je suis désolé(e), je n'ai pas de monnaie
Sorry, I don't have any change
zhuh swee day-zo-lay, zhuh nay pa duh mo-neh

Je suis pressé(e)
I'm in a hurry
zhuh swee preh-say

C'est loin?
Is it far?
say lwañ?

Chapter 10 Boat and ferry / Le bateau

À quelle heure part le prochain bateau/ferry pour...?
When is the next boat/ferry to...?
a kel ur par luh pro-shañ ba-toh/ feh-ree poor...?

Vous avez un horaire?
Have you a timetable?
voo za-vay uñ noh-rehr?

Est-ce qu'il y a un car ferry pour...?
Is there a car ferry to...?
es keel ya uñ car feh-ree poor...?

C'est combien...?
How much is...?
seh koñ-byañ...?

un aller simple
a single
uñ na-lay sañpl

un aller-retour
a return
uñ na-lay-ruh-toor

Un blllet touristique
A tourist ticket
uñ bee-yeh too-rees-teek

C'est combien pour une voiture et ... personnes?
How much is it for a car and ... people?
say koñ-byañ poor ewn vwa-tewr ay ... pehr-son?

La traversée dure combien de temps?
How long is the crossing?
la tra-vehr-say dewr koñ-byañ duh tahñ?

D'où part le bateau?
Where does the boat leave from?
doo par luh ba-toh?

Le premier/dernier bateau part quand?
When is the first/last boat?
luh pruh-myay/dehr-nyay ba-toh par kahñ?

On arrive à quelle heure à...?
What time do we get to...?
on a-reev a kel ur a...?

Est-ce qu'on peut manger sur le bateau?
Is there somewhere to eat on the boat?
es koñ puh mahñ-zhay sewr luh batoh?

Chapter 11 Air travel / Par avion

Comment fait-on pour aller à l'aéroport?
How do I get to the airport?
ko-mahñ fay toñ poor a-lay a la-ay-ro-por?

On met combien de temps pour aller à l'aéroport?
How long does it take to get to the airport?
oñ meh koñ-byañ duh tahñ poor a-lay a la-ay-ro-por?

C'est combien le taxi pour aller...?
How much is the taxi fare...?
say koñ-byañ luh tak-see poor alay...?

en ville
into town
ahñ veel

à l'hôtel
to the hotel
a loh-tel

Est-ce qu'il y a une navette pour aller au centre-ville?
Is there an airport bus to the city centre?
es keel ya ewn na-vet poor a-lay oh sahñtr-veel?

Où est l'enregistrement pour...?
Where do I check in for...?
oo ay lahñ-ruh-zhee-struh-mahñ poor...?

91

Où sont les bagages du vol en provenance de...?
Where is the luggage for the flight from...?
oo soñ lay ba-gazh dew vol ahñ pro-vnahñs duh...?

Quelle est la porte d'embarquement pour le vol à destination de...?
Which is the departure gate for the flight to...?
kel ay la port dahñ-bar-kuh-mahñ poor luh vol a des-tee-na-syoñ duh...?

L'embarquement aura lieu porte numéro...
Boarding will take place at gate number...
lahñ-bar-kuh-mahñ oh-ra lyuh port new-may-ro...

Présentez-vous immédiatement porte numéro...
Go immediately to gate number...
pray-zahñ-tay voo ee-maydyatmahñ port new-may-ro...

Votre vol a du retard
Your flight is delayed
votr vol a dew ruh-tar

Chapter 12 Customs control / Les douanes

contrôle des passeports
passport control
koñ-trol day pas-por

UE (Union Européenne)
EU (European Union)
ew uh

autres passeports
other passports
ohtr pas-por

douane
customs
doo-an

Est-ce que je dois payer des droits de douane sur ça?
Do I have to pay duty on this?
es kuh zhuh dwa pay-yay day drwa duh dwan sewr sa?

C'est pour mon usage personnel
It is for my own personal use
say poor moñ new-zazh pehr-so-nel

Nous allons en/au/aux...
We are on our way to...(if in transit through a country)
noo za-loñ ahñ/oh/oh...

Chapter 13 Petrol, gas/ l'essence

sans plomb
unleaded
sahñ ploñ

diesel/gasoil
diesel
dee-eh-zel/ga-zwal

Le plein, s'il vous plaît
Fill it up, please
luh plañ, seel voo pleh

Pouvez-vous vérifier l'huile/l'eau?
Please check the oil/the water
poo-vay voo vay-ree-fyay lweel/loh?

...euros d'essence sans plomb
...euros' worth of unleaded petrol
...uh-roh deh-sahñs sahñ ploñ

La pompe numéro...
Pump number...
la pomp new-may-roh...

Pouvez-vous vérifier la pression des pneus?
Can you check the tyre pressure?
Poo-vay voo vay-ree-fyay la preh-syoñ day pnuh?

94

Où dois-je payer?
Where do I pay?
oo dwa-zhuh pay-yay?

Vous acceptez les cartes de crédit?
Do you take credit cards?
voo zak-sep-tay lay kart duh kray-dee?

Chapter 14 Breakdown / Une panne

assistance automobile
breakdown assistance
a-sees-tahñs oh-toh-mo-beel

Pouvez-vous m'aider?
Can you help me?
poo-vay voo may-day?

Ma voiture est en panne
My car has broken down
ma vwa-tewr ay tahñ pan

Je n'arrive pas à démarrer
I can't start the car
zhuh na-reev pa a day-ma-ray

Je suis en panne d'essence
I've run out of petrol
zhuh swee ahñ pan deh-sahñs

Il y a un garage près d'ici?
Is there a garage near here?
eel ya uñ ga-razh preh dee-see?

Pouvez-vous me remorquer jusqu'au garage le plus proche?
Can you tow me to the nearest garage?
Poo-vay voo muh ruh-mor-kay zhew-skoh ga-razh luh plew prosh?

Avez-vous des pièces de rechange pour une...?
Do you have parts for a (make of car)?
a-vay voo day pyes duh ruh-shahñzh poor ewn...?

J'ai un problème avec le/la/les...
There's something wrong with the...
zhay uñ prob-lem a-vek luh/la/lay...

Chapter 15 Car parts / Les pièces détachées

Le/La/L' ... ne marche pas
The ... doesn't work
luh/la/l ... nuh marsh pa

Les ... ne marchent pas
The ... don't work
lay ... nuh marsh pa

l'accélérateur
accelerator
lak-say-lay-ra-tur

la batterie
battery
la ba-tree

le capot
bonnet
luh ka-poh

les freins
brakes
leh frañ

le starter
choke
luh star-tehr

l'embrayage
clutch
lahñ-bray-yazh

le delco
distributor
luh del-koh

le moteur
engine
luh mo-tur

le pot d'échappement
exhaust pipe
luh poh day-shapmahñ

le fusible
fuse
luh few-zeebl

les vitesses
gears
lay vee-tes

le frein à main
handbrake
luh frañ a mañ

les phares
headlights
lay far

l'allumage
ignition
la-lew-mazh

le clignotant
indicator
luh klee-nyo-tahñ

les vis platinées
points
lay vees pla-tee-nay

le radiateur
radiator
luh ra-dya-tur

les phares de recul
reversing lights
lay far duh ruh-kewl

la ceinture de sécurité
seat belt
la sañ-tewr duh say-kewr-eetay

les veilleuses
sidelights
lay vay-yuhz

la roue de secours
spare wheel
la roo duh skoor

les bougies
spark plugs
lay boo-zhee

la direction
steering
la dee-rek-syoñ

le volant
steering wheel
luh vo-lahñ

le pneu
tyre
luh pnuh

la roue
wheel
la roo

le pare-brise
windscreen
luh par-breez

le lave-glace
windscreen washers
luh lav-glas

l'essuie-glace
windscreen wiper
les-wee-glas

Chapter 16 Road signs / les panneaux de signalisation routière

Douane Zoll
Customs
Dwan zoll

Halte Peage
toll station for motorway
Al-tuh pai-ah-zhuh

Cedez Le Passage
give way
say-day luh pah-sahzh

Ralentir
slow down
ra-lon-teer

Sens Unique
one way
sahns oo-neek

Deviation
diversion priority road
dai-vee-a-see-on

Nord
North
nor

Sud
South
sood

Ouest
West
oo-aist

Est
East
aist

Libre
spaces
lee-bruh

Complet
full
kom-play

Stationnement Interdit
no parking
sta-see-on-mon an-tair-dee

Allumez Vos Feux
switch on your light
ay-loo-may voh fuh

Autoroute
motorway
o-toe-root

Chapter 17 Signs and notices / les panneaux

entrée
entrance
on-tray

sortie
exit
sor-tee

ouvert
open
oo-vair

fermé
closed
fair-may

chaud
hot
sho

froid
cold
frwa

tirez
pull
tee-ray

poussez
push
poo-say

à droite
right
ah drwat

à gauche
left
ah gosh

eau potable
drinking water
o po-tah-bluh

à emporter
take-away
ah on-por-tay

dégustation de vin
wine tasting
day-goos-tah-sion duh vahng

prière de...
please...
pree-yair duh

libre
free, vacant
lee-bruh

occupé
engaged
o-koo-pay

caisse
cash desk
kess

libre-service
self-service
lee-bruh sair-vees

toilettes
toilets
twa-let

dames
ladies
dam

hommes, messieurs
gents
om, may-syuh

hors service
out of order
or sair-vees

à louer
for hire/to rent
ah loo-ay

à vendre
for sale
ah von-druh

soldes
sale
sol-duh

baignade interdite
no bathing
bae-nyad an-tair-deet

sous-sol
basement
soo-sol

rez-de-chaussée
ground floor
ray-duh-shoh-say

ascenseur
lift
ah-son-suhr

accès aux trains
access to the trains
ak-say o tran

chambres
rooms available
shon-bruh

complet
no vacancies
kon-play

sortie de secours
emergency exit
sor-tee duh suh-koor

sonnez
ring
soh-nay

appuyez
press
ah-pwee-yay

privé
private
pree-vay

arrêt
stop
ah-ray

billets
tickets
bee-yay

accueil
information
ah-kuh-yuh

composter votre billet
validate your ticket
kom-pos-tay voh-truh bee-yay

buffet
snacks
boo-fay

consigne
left luggage
kon-see-nyuh

non fumeurs
non-smoking
non foo-muhr

fumeurs
smoking
foomuhr

défense de fumer
no smoking
day-fons duh foo-may

Part 4 : Leisure, Culture and Entertainment / Les loisirs, la culture et le divertissement

One of the wonderful aspects of learning a language is the cultural immersion and the experiences you gain from it. French culture has a wealth of connections to leisure and entertainment, which can really enhance your level of enjoyment when learning the language. When you take your interests, such as sports or the arts, and apply to them to learning French, you will find that you are more motivated and interested in increasing your knowledge about that topic while also learning the language along the way

Chapter 18 Sightseeing and tourist office - L'office du tourisme

Où est l'office de tourisme?
Where is the tourist office?
oo eh lo-fees duh too-reesm?

Qu'est-ce qu'il y a à voir dans la région?
What is there to visit in the area?
kes keel ya a vwar dahñ la ray-zhyoñ?

en … heures
in … hours
ahñ … ur

Avez-vous de la documentation?
Do you have any leaflets?
a-vay voo duh la do-kew-mahñ-ta-syoñ?

Est-ce qu'il y a des excursions?
Are there any excursions?
es keel ya day zek-skewr-syoñ?

On voudrait aller à...
We'd like to go to...
oñ voo-dreh a-lay a...

C'est combien l'entrée?
How much does it cost to get in?
say koñ-byañ lahñ-tray?

Est-ce que vous faites des reductions pour...?
Are there any reductions for...?
es kuh voo feht day ray-dewk-syoñ poor...?

les enfants
Children
lay zahñ-fahñ

les étudiants
students
lay zay-tew-dyahñ

112

les chômeurs
the unemployed
lay shoh-mur

les retraités
senior citizens
lay ruh-treh-tay

Chapter 19 Entertainment – Le divertissement

Qu'est-ce qu'on peut faire le soir?
What is there to do in the evenings?
kes koñ puh fehr luh swar?

Vous avez une liste des festivités pour ce mois-ci?
Do you have a list of events for this month?
Voo za-vay ewn leest day fes-tee-vee-tay poor suh mwa-see?

Est-ce qu'il y a des choses à faire pour les enfants?
Is there anything for children to do?
es keel ya day shohz a fehr poor lay zahñ- fahñ?

Où est-ce qu'on peut...?
Where can I/we...?
oo es koñ puh...?

pêcher
go fishing
peh-shay

faire du cheval
go riding
fehr dew shuh-val

114

Est-ce qu'il y a de bonnes plages (de sable) près d'ici?
Are there any good (sandy) beaches near here?
es keel ya duh bon plazh duh sabl preh dee-see?

Est-ce qu'il y a une piscine?
Is there a swimming pool?
es keel ya ewn pee-seen?

Chapter 20 Music – la musique

Il y a de bons concerts en ce moment?
Are there any good concerts on?
eel ya duh boñ koñ-sehr ahñ suh momahñ?

Où est-ce qu'on peut avoir des billets pour le concert?
Where can I get tickets for the concert?
oo es koñ puh av-war day bee-yeh poor luh koñ-sehr?

Où est-ce qu'on peut aller écouter de la musique classique/du jazz?
Where can we hear some classical music/some jazz?
oo es koñ puh a-lay ay-koo-tay duh la mew-zeek kla-seek/dew jaz?

Chapter 21 Cinema – le cinéma

sous-titré
subtitled
soo-tee-tray

la séance
performance
la sayahñs

VO (version originale)
in the original language (i.e. not dubbed)
vehr-syoñ o-ree-zhee-nal

Qu'est-ce qui passe au cinéma?
What's on at the cinema?
kes kee pas oh see-nay-ma?

Le film commence/finit à quelle heure?
When does the film start/finish?
luh feelm ko-mahñs/fee-nee a kel ur?

C'est combien les billets?
How much are the tickets?
say koñ-byañ lay bee-yeh?

Je voudrais deux places à ... euros
I'd like two seats at ... euros
zhuh voo-dreh duh plas a ... uh-roh

117

Chapter 22 Theater/opera – le théâtre et l'opéra

la pièce
play
la pyes

la représentation
performance
la ruh-pray-zahñ-ta-syoñ

à l'orchestre
in the stalls
a lor-kestr

au balcon
in the circle
oh bal-koñ

le fauteuil
seat
luh foh-tuh-yuh

le vestiaire
cloakroom
luh ves-tyehr

l'entracte
interval
lahñ-trakt

Qu'est-ce qu'on joue au théâtre/à l'opéra?
What is on at the theatre/at the opera?
kes koñ zhoo oh tay-atr/a lo-pay-ra?

Les billets sont à combien?
What prices are the tickets?
lay bee-yeh soñ ta koñ-byañ?

Je voudrais deux billets...
I'd like two tickets...
zhuh voo-dreh duh bee-yeh...

pour ce soir
for tonight
poor suh swar

pour demain soir
for tomorrow night
poor duh-mañ swar

pour le cinq août
for 5th August
poor luh sañk oo(t)

Quand est-ce que la représentation commence/finit?
When does the performance begin/end?
kahñ tes kuh la ruh-pray-zahñ-ta-syoñ ko-mahñs/fee-nee?

Chapter 23 Television – la télévision

la télécommande
remote control
la tay-lay-ko-mahñd

le feuilleton
soap
luh fuh-yuh-toñ

les informations
news
lay zañ-for-ma-syoñ

mettre en marche
to switch on
metr ahñ marsh

éteindre
to switch off
ay-tañdr

les dessins animés
cartoons
lay deh-sañ a-nee-may

Où est la télévision?
Where is the television?
oo ay la tay-lay-vee-zyoñ?

Comment la met-on en marche?
How do you switch it on?
ko-mahñ la meh toñ ahñ marsh?

Qu'est-ce qu'il y a à la télé?
What is on television?
kes keel ya a la tay-lay?

Les informations sont à quelle heure?
When is the news?
lay zañ-for-ma-syoñ soñ ta kel ur?

Est-ce qu'il y a des chaînes en anglais?
Do you have any English-language channels?
es keel ya day shen ahñ nahñ-gleh?

Avez-vous des vidéos en anglais?
Do you have any English videos?
a-vay voo day vee-day-o ahñ nahñ-gleh?

121

Chapter 24 Sports – le sport

Où est-ce qu'on peut…?
Where can I/we…?
oo es koñ puh…?

jouer au tennis
play tennis
zhoo-ay oh teh-nees

jouer au golf
play golf
zhoo-ay oh golf

faire de la natation
go swimming
fehr duh la na-ta-syoñ

faire du jogging
go jogging
fehr dew jo-geeng

C'est combien l'heure?
How much is it per hour?
say koñ-byañ lur?

Est-ce qu'il faut être membre?
Do you have to be a member?
es keel foh (t)etr mahñbr?

Est-ce qu'on peut louer...?
Can we hire...?
es koñ puh loo-ay...?

des raquettes
Rackets
day ra-ket

des clubs de golf
golf clubs
day club duh golf

Nous voudrions aller voir jouer l'équipe de...
We'd like to go to see (name of team) play
noo voo-dryoñ a-lay vwar zhoo-ay laykeep duh...

Où est-ce qu'on peut avoir des billets?
Where can I/we get tickets?
oo es koñ puh a-vwar day bee-yeh?

Qu'est-ce que vous faites comme sports?
What sports do you play?
kes kuh voo fet kom spor?

Il n'y a plus de billets pour le match
There are no tickets left for the game
eel nya plew duh bee-yeh poor luh match

Chapter 25 Walking – la promenade

Y a-t-il des promenades guidées?
Are there any guided walks?
ee ya-teel day prom-nad gee-day?

Avez-vous un guide des promenades dans la région?
Do you have a guide to local walks?
a-vay vooz uñ geed day prom-nad dahñ la ray-zhyoñ?

Vous connaissez de bonnes promenades?
Do you know any good walks?
voo ko-neh-say duh bon prom-nad?

La promenade fait combien de kilomètres?
How many kilometres is the walk?
la prom-nad feh koñ-byañ duh kee-lo-metr?

Ça prendra combien de temps?
How long will it take?
sa prahñ-dra koñ-byañ duh tahñ?

Est-ce que ça monte dur?
Is it very steep?
es kuh sa moñt dewr?

Nous aimerions faire de l'escalade
We'd like to go climbing
noo zeh-muh-ryoñ fehr duh les-ka-lad

Chapter 26 Phone and Text messaging – Téléphone et l'envoi de sms

Je voudrais téléphoner
I'd like to make a phone call
zhuh voo-dreh tay-lay-fo-nay

Il y a un téléphone public?
Is there a pay phone?
eel ya uñ tay-lay-fon pew-bleek?

Une télécarte, s'il vous plaît
A phonecard, please
ewn tay-lay-kart, seel voo pleh

de ... euros
for ... euros
duh ... uh-roh

Vous avez un portable?
Do you have a mobile?
voo za-vay uñ por-tabl?

Quel est le numéro de votre portable?
What's your mobile number?
kel eh luh new-may-ro duh votr por-tabl?

Je peux emprunter votre portable?
Can I use your mobile?
zhuh puh ahñ-pruñ-tay votr por-tabl?

Le numéro de mon portable est le...
My mobile number is...
luh new-may-ro duh moñ por-tabl ay luh...

Âllo?
Hello
alo?

C'est de la part de qui?
Who's calling?
say duh la par duh kee?

De la part de...
This is...
duh la par duh...

Un instant, s'il vous plaît...
Just a moment...
uñ nañ-stahñ seel voo pleh...

Pourrais-je parler à...?
Can I speak to...?
poo-rezh par-lay a ...?

... à l'appareil
It's (your name)
... a la-pa-ray

Comment on fait pour avoir une ligne extérieure?
How do I get an outside line?
ko-mahñ oñ feh poor a-vwar ewn leen-yuh ekstay-
ree-ur?

Je vous rappellerai…
I'll call back…
zhuh voo ra-pel-ray…

plus tard
later
plew tar

demain
tomorrow
duh-mañ

Je vous le/la passe
I'm putting you through
zhuh voo luh/la pas

C'est occupé
It's engaged
say to-kew-pay

Pouvez-vous rappeler plus tard?
Please try later?
poo-vay voo ra-play plew tar?

Voulez-vous laisser un message?
Do you want to leave a message?
voo-lay voo leh-say uñ meh-sazh?

Veuillez laisser votre message après le bip sonore
Please leave a message after the tone
vuh-yay lay-say votr meh-sazh a-preh luh beep so-nor

S'il vous plaît, éteignez votre portable
Please turn your mobile off
seel voo pleh, ay-ten-yay votr por-tabl

Je t'enverrai un message
I will text you
zhuh tahñ-veh-ray uñ meh-sazh

Tu peux m'envoyer un message?
Can you text me?
tew puh mahñ-vwa-yay uñ meh-sazh?

Chapter 27 E-mail – le courriel

Nouveau message:
New message:

A:
To:

De:
From:

Objet:
Subject:

CC:
CC:

Pièce jointe:
Attachment:

Envoyer:
Send:

Vous avez une adresse e-mail?
Do you have an e-mail address?
voo za-vay ewn a-dres ee-mehl?

Quelle est votre adresse e-mail?
What's your e-mail address?
kel ay votr a-dres ee-mehl?

Comment ça s'écrit?
How do you spell it?
ko-mahñ sa say-kree?

En un seul mot
All in one word
ahñ uñ suhl moh

Tout en minuscules
All lower case
too tahñ mee-new-skewl

Mon adresse e-mail est...
My e-mail address is...
moñ nad-res ee-mehl ay...

xx point xx arobase ... point CO point UK point COM
XX.XX@(company name).co.uk /.com
xx pwañ xx a-roh-baz ... pwañ say oh pwañ ew ka / pwan come

Je peux envoyer un e-mail?
Can I send an e-mail?
zhuh puh ahñ-vwa-yay uñ nee-mehl?

Est-ce que vous avez reçu mon e-mail?
Did you get my e-mail?
es-kuh voo za-vay ruh-sew moñ nee-mehl?

130

Chapter 28 Internet

accueil
home
a-kuh-yuh

nom d'utilisateur
username
noñ dew-tee-lee-za-tur

moteur de recherche
search engine
mo-tur duh ruh-shehrsh

mot de passe
password
moh duh pas

contactez-nous
contact us
koñ-tak-tay-noo

retour vers le sommaire
back to menu
ruh-toor vehr luh som-mehr

Est-ce qu'il y a des cybercafés par ici?
Are there any internet cafés here?
es keel ya day see-behr-ka-fay par eesee?

Combien coûte une heure de connexion?
How much is it to log on for an hour?
koñ-byañ koot ewn ur duh ko-neksyoñ?

Je n'arrive pas à me connecter
I can't log on
zhuh na-reev pa a muh ko-nek-tay

Chapter 29 Fax

À/De
To/From

Objet :
Re:

Nombre de pages
Number of pages

Veuillez trouver ci-joint...
Please find attached...

Avez-vous un fax?
Do you have a fax?
a-vay voo uñ fax?

Je voudrais envoyer un fax
I want to send a fax
zhuh voo-dreh ahñ-vwa-yay uñ fax

Quel est votre numéro de fax?
What is your fax number?
kel ay votr new-may-roh duh fax?

Mon numéro de fax est le...
My fax number is...
moñ new-may-roh duh fax ay luh...

Part 5 : Eating and Drinking – Manger et boire

One of the best ways to enjoy life is to indulge in food and drink. It is a happy occurrence when you are able to do this while learning a language. Once you have learned some basic French vocabulary and phrases related to eating and drinking, you can reward yourself with a trip to a French restaurant or café to put these skills to good use. Even better, if you get the chance to go to a French speaking country, you will find that this vocabulary comes in very handy.

Chapter 30 Café / Restaurant Drink / Food - La nourriture

Le barman
The bartender
luh bar-mahn

Une boisson
A drink
ewn bwahsawn

Un jus de fruit
A fruit drink
uhn zhew duhfrwee

Une boisson gazeuse
A soft drink
ewn bwahsawn ga-zuhz

Une bouteille d'eau minérale
A bottle of mineral water
ewn boo-tay doh mee-nay-ral

Un verre de porto
A glass of porto
uhn vuhr duh pawr-toh

De la bière (blonde, brune)
Some beer (light, dark)
duh la byehr (blawnd, brewn)

Du vin (rouge, blanc)
Some wine (red, white)
dew van (roozh, blahn)

Prenons-en un autre
let's have another
pruh-nawn zahn uh NOH-truh

A votre santé!
To your health!
ah VAW-truh sahn-tay!

Chapter 31 At the restaurant / Au restaurant

Où peut-on trouver un bon restaurant?
Where is there a good restaurant?
oo puh-tawn troo-vay uhn bawn ress-taw-rawn ?

Est-ce que vous pouvez me conseiller …?
Can you recommend …?
es-ke voo poo-vey me kon-sey-yey …

un bar
a bar
um bar

un café
a café
ung ka-fey

un restaurant
a restaurant
un res-to-ron

Je voudrais …,s'il vous plaît.
I'd like …, please
zhe voo-drey …seel voo pley

une table pour (cinq) personnes
a table for (five)
ewn ta-ble poor (sungk) pair-son

un endroit pour (non-)fumeurs
the (non)smoking section
un on-drwa poor non-few-muhr

Qu'est-ce que vous conseillez?
What would you recommend?
kes-ke voo kon-sey-yey

Je voudrais …,s'il vous plaît.
I'd like …,please.
zhe voo-drey …seel voo pley

l'addition
the bill
la-dee-syon

la carte des boissons
the drink list
la kart dey bwa-son

la carte
the menu
la kart

ce plat
that dish
suh pla

la carte des vins
the wine list
la kart dey vun

Le petit déjeuner
Breakfast
luh puh-tee day-zhuh-nay

Le déjeuner
Lunch
luh day-zhuh-nay

Le dîner
Dinner
luh dee-nay

Le souper
Supper
luh soo-pay

Un sandwich
A sandwich
uhn sahnd-weetsh

Un casse-croûte
A snack
uhn kass-kroot

À quelle heure servez-vous le dîner?
At what time is dinner served?
ah keh luhr sehr-vay-voo luh dee-nay?

Pouvons-nous déjeuner (diner) maintenant?
Can we have lunch (dinner) now?
poo-vaum-noo day-zhuh-nay (dee-nay) ment-nahn?

La serveuse
The waitress
la sehr-vuhz

Le garçon
The waiter
luh gar-saum

Le maître d'hôtel
The headwaiter
luh MEH-truh doh-tel

Garçon!
Waiter!
garsawn!

Nous sommes deux
There are two of us
noo sawm duh

Donnez-moi une table près de la fenêtre
Give me a table near the window
daw-nay-mwah ewn TA-bluh preh duh la fuh-NEH-truh

Nous voulons dîner à la carte
We want to dine à la carte
noo voo-lawn dee-nay ah la kart

À prix fixe
Table
ah pree feeks

Servez-nous vite, s'il vous plaît
Please serve us quickly
sehr-vay-noo veet, seel voo pleh

Apportez-moi le menu
Bring me the menu
ap-pawr-tay-mwah luh muh-new

Une fourchette
A fork
Ewn foor-shet

Un couteau
A knife
uhn koo-toh

Une assiette
A plate
ewn as-syet

Une cuillère à café
A teaspoon
ewn kwee-yeh rah ka-fay

Une cuillère à soupe
A tablespoon
ewn kwee-yeh rah soop

la tasse
the cup
lah tass

Je désire quelque chose de simple
I want something simple
zhuh day-zeer kel-kuh shohz duh SEN-pluh

Pas trop épicé
Not too spicy
pah troh pay-pee-say

J'aime la viande saignante
I like the meat rare
zhem la vee-ahnd sayn-yahnt

Bien cuite
Well done
byen kweet

Emportez cela, s'il vous plaît
Take it away, please
ahn-pawr-tay suh-la, seel voo pleh

C'est froid
This is cold
Seh frwah

Je n'ai pas commandé cela
I did not order this
zhuh nay pah kaw-mahn-day suh-la

Pouvez-vous remplacer cela par une salade?
May i change this for a salad?
poo-vay-voo rahn-plasay suh-la par ewn sa-lad?

L'addition, s'il vous plaît
The check, please
la-dee-syawn, seel voo pleh

Le pourboire, est-il compris?
Is the tip included?
luh poor-bwahr, eh-teel kawn-pree?

Le service, est-il compris?
Is the service charge included?
luh sehr-veess, eh-teel kawn-pree?

Il y a une erreur dans l'addition
There is a mistake in the bill
eelya ewn ehr-ruhr dahn la-dee-syawn

Pourquoi ces suppléments?
What are these charges for?
poor-kwah say sew-play-mahn?

Gardez la monnaie
Keep the change
gar-day la maw-neh

La cuisine et le service étaient excellents
The food and service were excellent
la kwee-zeen ay luh sehr-veess ay-teh tex-eh-lahn

L'eau potable
Drinking water
loh paw-TA-bluh

Avec de la glace
With ice
a-vek duh la glas

le dessert
the dessert
luh desair

le poisson
the fish
luh pwasson

la fourchette
the fork
la foorshet

le verre
the glass
luh vair

le couteau
the knife
luh kooto

le plat principal
the main course
luh pla pranseepal

la viande
the meat
la veeond

la carte
the menu
la kart

le poivre
pepper
luh pwahvr

l'assiette
the plate
lass-yet

la salade
the salad
la sa-lad

le sel
salt
luh cell

le menu (à prix fixe)
the set menu
luh muhnOO (a pree feex)

le potage
the soup
luh potahj

la cuillère
the spoon
la kwee-yair

l'entrée
starter
lontray

la table
the table
la tahbl

encore ..., s'il vous plaît
another ..., please
onkor ..., seel voo play

pardon
excuse me! (to call waiter/waitress)
par-don

l'addition, s'il vous plaît
could I have the bill, please?
ladeess-yon seel voo play

Quelle est la spécialité locale?
What's the local speciality?
kel ey la spey-sya-lee-tey lo-kal

Qu'est-ce que c'est, ça?
What's that?
kes-ke sey sa

Sans glace
Without ice
sahn glas

Chapter 32 Foods / La nourriture

Le pain
The bread
luh pehn

Le beurre
The butter
luh buhr

Le sucre
The sugar
luh sew-kruh

Le sel
The salt
luh sel

Le poivre
The pepper
luh pwah-vruh

La sauce
The sauce
la sohss

L'huile
The oil
lweel

Le vinaigre
The vinegar
luh vee-neh-gruh

La moutarde
The mustard
la moo-tard

L'ail
The garlic
Lahyuh

Du poulet rôti
Some roast chicken
dew poo-leh roh-tee

Du poulet frit
Some fried chicken
dew poo-leh free

Du boeuf
Some beef
dew buhf

Du canard
Some duck
dew ka-nar

De l'oie
Some goose
duh lwah

Du gigot
Some lamb
dew zhee-goh

Du foie
Some liver
Dew fwah

Du homard
Some lobster
dew aw-mar

Du porc
Some pork
Dew pawr

Du rosbif
Some roast beef
dew raws-beef

Des sardines
Some sardines
day sar-deen

Du bifteck
Some steak
dew bif-tek

Des crevettes
Some shrimps
day kruh-vet

De la saucisse
Some sausage
duh la saw-sees

Du veau
Some veal
dew voh

baba au rhum
small sponge cake, often with raisins, soaked in a
rum-flavoured syrup
ba-ba o rom

béarnaise f
white sauce of wine or vinegar beaten with egg yolks
& flavoured with herbs
bey-ar-neyz

blanquette de veau f
veal stew in white sauce with cream
blong-ket de vo

bombe glacée f
ice cream with candied fruits, glazed chestnuts &
cream
bom-be gla-sey

bouillabaisse f
fish soup stewed in a broth with garlic, orange peel,
fennel, tomatoes & saffron
bwee-ya-bes

brioche f
small roll or cake sometimes flavoured with nuts, currants or candied fruits
bree-yosh

brochette f
grilled skewer of meat or vegetables
bro-shet

consommé m
clarified meat or fish-based broth
kon-so-mey

contre-filet m
beef sirloin roast
kon-tre-fee-ley

coulis m
fruit or vegetable purée, used as a sauce
koo-lee

croque-madame m
grilled or fried ham & cheese sandwich,topped with a fried egg
krok-ma-dam

croquembouche m
cream puffs dipped in caramel
kro-kom-boosh

croque-monsieur m
grilled or fried ham & cheese sandwich
krok-mes-yeu

croustade f
puff pastry filled with fish, seafood, meat, mushrooms
or vegetables
kroo-stad

dijonnaise
dishes with a mustard-based sauce
dee-zho-nez

estouffade f
meat stewed in wine with carrots & herbs
es-too-fad

friand m
pastry stuffed with minced sausage meat, ham &
cheese, or almond cream
free-yon

fricandeau m
veal fillet simmered in white wine, vegetables herbs &
spices / a pork pâté
free-kon-do

fricassée f
lamb, veal or poultry in a thick creamy sauce with
mushrooms & onions
free-ka-sey

grenadin m
veal (or sometimes poultry) fillet, wrapped in a thin slice of bacon
gre-na-dun

michette f
savoury bread stuffed with cheese, olives, onions & anchovies
mee-shet

pain-bagnat m
small round bread loaves, filled with onions, vegetables, anchovies & olives
pun ban-ya

plateau de fromage m
cheese board or platter
pla-to de fro-mazh

pomme duchesse f
fritter of mashed potato, butter & egg yolk
pom dew-shes

pot-au-feu m
beef, root vegetable & herb stockpot
po-to-fe

potée f
meat & vegetables cooked in a pot
po-tey

profiterole m
small pastry with savoury or sweet fillings
pro-fee-trol

puits d'amour m
puff pastry filled with custard or jam
pwee da-moor

quenelle f
fish or meat dumpling, often poached
ke-nel

quiche f
tart with meat, fish or vegetable filling
keesh

raclette f
hot melted cheese, served with potatoes & gherkins
ra-klet

ragoût m
stew of meat, fish and/or vegetables
ra-goo

ratatouille f
vegetable stew
ra-ta-too-ye

roulade f
slice of meat or fish rolled around stuffing
roo-lad

savarin m
sponge cake soaked with a rum syrup & filled with custard, cream & fruits
sa-va-run

savoie f
light cake made with beaten egg whites
sav-wa

tartiflette f
dish of potatoes, cheese & bacon
tar-tee-flet

velouté m
rich, creamy soup, usually prepared with vegetables, shellfish or fish purée
vew-loo-tay

vol-au-vent m
puff pastry filled with a mixture of sauce & meat, seafood or vegetables
vo-lo-von

Chapter 33 Menu breakfast foods / Le petit-déjeuner

Puis-je avoir du jus de fruit?
May I bave some fruit juice?
PWEE-zhuh a-vwahr dew zhew duhfrwee?

Du jus d'orange
Some orange juice
dew zhew daw-rahnzh

Des pruneaux cuits
Some stewed prunes
day prew-noh kwee

Du jus de tomate
Some tomato juice
dew zhew duh taw-maht

Des toasts avec de la confiture
Some toast and jaw
day tohst a-vek duh la kawn-fet-tewr

Des petits pains
Some rolls
day puh-tee pen

Une omelette
an omelet
ewn awm-let

Des oeufs à la coque
Some soft-boiled eggs
day zuh ah la kawk

Des oeufs quatre minutes
Some medium boiled eggs
day zhuh KA-truh mee-newt

Des oeufs durs
Some hard-boiled eggs
day zuh dewr

Des oeufs sur le plat
Some fried egg
day zuh sewr luh pla

Des œufs brouillés
Some scrambled eggs
day zuh broo-yay

Des oeufs avec du lard
Some bacon and eggs
day zuh a-vek dew lar

Des oeufs au jambon
Some ham and eggs
day zuh oh zhawn-bawn

Chapter 34 Special Diets & Allergies / Les régimes alimentaires et allergies

Y a-t-il un restaurant végétarien par ici?
Is there a vegetarian restaurant near here?
ya-teel un res-to-ron vey-zhey-ta-ryun par ee-see

Vous faites les repas végétarien?
Do you have vegetarian food?
voo fet ley re-pa vey-zhey-ta-ryun

Pouvez-vous préparer un repas sans ...?
Could you prepare a meal without ...?
poo-vey-voo prey-pa-rey un re-pa son ...

beurre
butter
beur

œufs
eggs
zeu

bouillon gras
meat stock
boo-yon gra

Je suis allergique ...
I'm allergic ...
zhe swee za-lair-zheek ...

aux produits laitiers
to dairy produce
o pro-dwee ley-tyey

au gluten
to gluten
o glew-ten

au glutamate de sodium
to MSG
o glew-ta-mat de so-dyom

au noix
to nuts
oh nwa

aux fruits de mer
to seafood
oh frwee de mair

Chapter 35 Soups and entrées / Soupes et entrées

Je désire du potage au poulet
I want some chicken soup
zhuh day-zeer dew paw-tazh oh poo-leh

Du potage aux légumes
Some vegetable soup
dew paw-tazh oh lay-gewm

Chapter 36 Vegetables and salad / Légumes et salades

Je désire des asperges
I want some asparagus
zhuh day-zeer day zas-pehrzh

Des carottes
Some carrots
day ka-rawt

Du chou
Some cabbage
dew shoo

Des haricots
Some beans
day a-ri-koh

Du chou-fleur
Some cauliflower
dew shoo-fluhr

Du céleri et-des olives
Some celery and olives
dew sayl-ree ay day zaw-leev

Du concombre
Some cucumber
dew kawn-kawn-bruh

De la laitue
Some letuce
duh la leh-tew

Des champignons
Some mushrooms
day shahn-peen-yawn

Des oignons
Some onions
day zawn-yawn

Des petits pois
Some peas
day puh-tee pwah

Des poivrons
Some peppers
day pwahv-rawn

Des pommes de terre bouillies
Some boiled potatoes
day pawm duh tehr boo-yee

Des pommes de terre frites
Some fried potatoes
day pawm duh tehr freet

De la purée de pommes de terre
Some mashed potatoes
duh la pew-ray duh pawm duh tehr

Du riz
Some rice
dew ree

Des épinards
Some spinach
day zay-pee-nahr

Des tomates
Some tomatoes
day taw-maht

Chapter 37 Fruits

Je désire une pomme
I want an apple
zhuh day-zee rewn pawm

Des cerises
Some cherries
day suh-reez

Une pamplemousse
A grapefruit
ewn pahn-pluh-mooss

Du raisin
Some grapes
dew ray-zen

Du citron
Some lemon
dew see trawn

Du melon
Some melon
dew muh-lawn

Des noix
Some nuts
day nwah

Une orange
an orange
ew naw-rahnzh

Une pêche
A peach
ewn pesh

Des framboises
A raspberries
Day frahn-bwahz

Des fraises
Some strawberries
day frayz

Chapter 38 Beverages & Drinks / Les boissons

Du café noir
Some black coffee
dew ka-fay nwahr

Un café crème
Coffee with cream
uhn ka-fay kraym

Du lait
Some milk
dew leh

Du thé
Some tea
dew tay

De la citronnade
Some lemonade
duh la see-traw-nad

la bière
beer
la bee-air

la bouteille
the bottle
la bootay

166

le gin
gin
luh djeen

le lait
milk
luh lay

l'eau minérale f
mineral water
lo meenayral

le jus d'orange
orange juice
luh joo doronj

le porto
port
luh portoh

le vin rouge
red wine
luh van rooj

le rosé
rosé
luh rozzay

la boisson non-alcoolisée
soft drink
la bwasson non-alkoleezay

le sucre
sugar
luh sookr

le thé
tea
luh tay

l'eau
water
lo

le vin blanc
white wine
luh van blon

le vin
wine
luh van

la carte des vins
wine list
la kart day van

alcool
alcohol
alkool

bière (à la) pression
draught beer
bee-air press-yon

bière brune
bitter; dark beer
bee-air broon

bière rousse
relatively sweet, fairly dark beer
bee-air rooss

blanc
white wine; white
blon

blanc de blancs
white wine from white grapes
blon duh blon

blanquette de Limoux
sparkling white wine from Languedoc
blonket duh leemoo

Bourgogne
wine from the Burgundy area
boor-goh-nyuh

Brouilly
red wine from the Beaujolais area
broo-yee

brut
very dry
brOOt

café
espresso, very strong black coffee
kafay

café au lait
white coffee
kafay o lay

café crème
white coffee
kafay krem

café glacé
iced coffee
kafay glassay

café soluble
instant coffee
kafay soloobl

café viennois
coffee with whipped cream
kafay vee-enwa

thé à la camomille
camomile tea
tay ah la kamomee

capiteux
heady
kapeetuh

carte des vins
wine list
kart day van

Chablis
dry white wine from Burgundy
shablee

chambré
at room temperature
shonbray

Champagne
champagne
Shonpah-nyuh

champagnisé
sparkling
shonpan-yeezay

chartreuse
herb liqueur
shartrurz

Château-Margaux
red wine from the Bordeaux area
shato margo

Châteauneuf-du-Pape
red wine from the Rhône valley
shatonurf doo pap

chocolat chaud
hot chocolate
shokola sho

chocolat glacé
iced chocolate drink
shokola glassay

cidre
cider
seedr

cidre bouché
cider in bottle with a cork
seedr booshay

cidre doux
sweet cider
seedr doo

51® (cinquante-et-un)
a brand of pastis
sankontay-an

citron pressé
fresh lemon juice
seetron pressay

cognac
brandy
konyak

crème
white coffee
krem

crème de cassis
blackcurrant liqueur
krem duh kasseess

cru
vintage
kroo

décaféiné
decaffeinated
daykafay-eenay

demi
small draught beer; quarter of a litre of beer
duhmee

demi-sec
medium dry
duhmee-sek

diabolo menthe/fraise etc
mint/strawberry etc cordial with lemonade
d-yabolo mont/frez

digestif
liqueur
deejesteef

eau
water
o

eau de vie
spirit made from fruit
o duh vee

eau minérale
mineral water
o meenayral

eau minérale gazeuse
sparkling mineral water
o meenayral gazurz

Fendant
Swiss dry white wine
fondon

fine
fine brandy, liqueur brandy
feen

Fleurie
red wine from Beaujolais
flurree

frappé
well chilled, on ice; iced
frapay

gazeux
fizzy
gazur

Gewurztraminer
dry white wine from Alsace
guh-woorztrameenair

glaçon
ice cube
glasson

grand crème
large white coffee
gron krem

grand cru
fine vintage
gron kroo

Graves
red wine from the Bordeaux area
Grahv

infusion
herb tea
anfOOz-yon

jus
juice
jOO

jus de pommes
apple juice
jOO duh pom

jus d'orange
orange juice
jOO doronj

lait
milk
lay

lait fraise/grenadine
milk with strawberry/grenadine cordial
lay frez/gruhnadeen

limonade
lemonade
leemonad

Mâcon
wine from Burgundy
makon

marc
clear spirit distilled from grape pulp
mar

Médoc
red wine from the Bordeaux area
Maydok

176

menthe à l'eau
mint cordial
mont a lo

Meursault
wine from Burgundy
murrso

millésime
vintage
meelay-zeem

mousseux
sparkling
moossuh

Muscadet
dry white wine from the Nantes area
mooskaday

muscat
sweet white wine
mooska

Noilly-Prat®
an aperitif wine similar to Dry Martini
nwa-yee pra

Nuits-Saint-Georges
red wine from Burgundy
nwee San jorj

orange pressée
fresh orange juice
oronj pressay

panaché
shandy
panashay

Passe-Tout-Grain
red wine from Burgundy
pass too gran

pastis
aniseed-flavoured alcoholic drink
pasteess

Pernod
a brand of pastis
Pairno

pétillant
sparkling
paytee-on

Pouilly-Fuissé
dry white wine from Burgundy
poo-yee-fweessay

premier cru
vintage wine
pruhm-yay croo

pression
draught beer, draught
press-yon

rhum
rum
rom

Ricard®
a brand of pastis
reekar

rosé
rosé wine
rozzay

rouge
red
rooj

Saint-Amour
red wine from Beaujolais
santamoor

Saint-Emilion
red wine from the Bordeaux area
san-taymcclee-yon

Sauternes
fruity white wine from the Bordeaux area
sotairn

sec
dry; neat
sek

sirop
cordial
seero

thé
tea
tay

thé à la menthe
mint tea
tay ah la mont

thé au lait
tea with milk
tay o lay

thé citron
lemon tea
tay seetron

thé nature
tea without milk
tay natoor

tilleul
lime-flower tea
tee-yurl

thé à la verveine
verbena tea
tay ah la vairven

vin
wine
Van

vin blanc
white wine
Van blon

vin de pays
regional wine
Van duh payee

vin de table
table wine
Van duh tahbl

vin rosé
rosé wine
Van rozzay

vin rouge
red wine
Van rooj

Yvorne
Swiss dry white wine
eevorn

(un) café ...
(cup of) coffee ...
(ung) ka-fey ...

(un) thé ...
(cup of) tea ...
(un) tey ...

au lait
with milk
o ley

sans sucre
without sugar
son sew-kre

eau ...
... water
o...

chaude
hot
shod

minérale gazeuse
sparkling mineral
mee-ney-ral ga-zeuz

minérale non-gazeuse
still mineral
mee-ney-ral nong-ga-zeuz

182

Chapter 39 Beverages & Drinks / Les boissons part 2

Je prends …
I'll have …
zhe pron …

Je vous offre un verre.
I'll buy you a drink.
zhe voo zo-fre un vair

Qu'est-ce que vous voulez?
What would you like?
kes-ke voo voo-ley

Santé!
Cheers!
son-tey

cognac m
brandy
ko-nyak

champagne m
champagne
shom-pan-ye

cocktail m
cocktail
kok-tel

un petit verre de (whisky)
a shot of (whisky)
um pe-tee vair de (wees-kee)

une bouteille de vin ...
a bottle of ... wine
ewn boo-tey de vun ...

un verre de vin ...
a glass of ... wine
un vair de vun ...

rouge
red
roozh

mousseux
sparkling
moo-seu

blanc
white
blong

... de bière
... of beer
... de byair

une bouteille
a bottle
ewn boo-tey

Chapter 40 Desserts – Les desserts

Puis-je avoir du gâteau?
May I have some cake?
Pwee-zhah-vwahr dew gah-toh?

Du fromage
Some cheese
dewfraw-mazh

De petits gâteaux secs
Some cookies
duh puh-tee gah-toh sek

Des crêpes Suzette
Some crêpes
day krep sew-zet

De la crème renversée
Some custard
duh la krem rahn-vehr-say

De la glace au chocolat
Some chocolate ice cream
duh la glas oh shaw-kaw-la

De la glace à la vanille
Some ice vanilla
duh la glas ah la va-NEE-yuh

Chapter 41 Bar/café

un (café) crème
white creamy coffee
uñ (ka-fay) krem

un grand crème
large white creamy coffee
uñ grahñ krem

un café au lait
coffee with hot milk
uñ ka-fay oh leh

un café
a coffee
uñ ka-fay

une orangeade
an orangeade
ewn o-rahñ-zhad

au citron
with lemon
oh see-troñ

sans sucre
no sugar
sahñ sewkr

pour deux personnes
for two
poor duh pehr-son

pour moi
for me
poor mwa

pour lui/elle
for him/her
poor lwee/el

pour nous
for us
poor noo

avec des glaçons, s'il vous plaît
with ice, please
a-vek day gla-soñ, seel voo pleh

De l'eau minérale...
Some ... mineral water
duh loh mee-nay-ral...

gazeuse
sparkling
ga-zuhz

plate
still
plat

Chapter 42 Reading the menu - Lire un menu

Plat du jour à 7 € 50 – poisson ou viande ou volaille garnis
Dish of the day 7 € 50 - fish or meat or poultry with veg and French fries.

menu du midi – entrée + plat + café
lunchtime menu – starter + main course + coffee.

Chapter 43 In a restaurant – dans un restaurant

Qu'est-ce que vous prenez?
What will you have?
kes kuh voo pruh-nay?

Un thé au lait, s'il vous plaît
A tea with milk, please
uñ tay oh leh, seel voo pleh

Je voudrais réserver une table pour ... personnes
I'd like to book a table for ... people
zhuh voo-dreh ray-zehr-vay ewn tabl poor ... pehr-son

Pour ce soir/pour demain soir/pour dix-neuf heures trente
For tonight/for tomorrow night/for 7.30
poor suh swar/poor duh-mañ swar/poor deez-nuh vur trahñt

Une table pour deux?
A table for two?
ewn tabl poor duh?

Le menu, s'il vous plaît
The menu, please
luh muh-new, seel voo pleh

Part 5 : Eating and Drinking – Manger et boire

Quel est le plat du jour?
What is the dish of the day?
kel eh luh pla dew zhoor?

Je prends le menu à …euros, s'il vous plaît
I'll have the menu at … euros, please
zhuh prahñ luh muh-new a …uh-roh, seel voo pleh

Pouvez-vous nous recommander un plat régional?
Can you recommend a local dish?
poo-vay voo noo ruh-ko-mahñ-day uñ pla ray-zhyo-nal?

Qu'est-ce qu'il y a dedans?
What is in this?
kes keel ya duh-dahñ?

Je prends ça
I'll have this
zhuh prahñ sa

Encore du pain…
More bread…
ahñ-kor dew pañ…

Encore de l'eau…
More water…
ahñ-kor duh loh…

s'il vous plaît
please
seel voo pleh

L'addition, s'il vous plaît
The bill, please
la-dee-syoñ, seel voo pleh

Est-ce que le service est compris?
Is service included?
es kuh luh sehr-vees ay koñ-pree?

Chapter 44 Vegetarian / végétarien

Est-ce qu'il y a des restaurants végétariens ici?
Are there any vegetarian restaurants here?
es keel ya day res-toh-rahñ vay-zhay-ta-ryañ ee-see?

Vous avez des plats végétariens?
Do you have any vegetarian dishes?
voo za-vay day pla vay-zhay-ta-ryañ?

Quels sont les plats sans viande/poisson?
Which dishes have no meat/fish?
kel soñ lay plah sahñ vyahñd/pwasoñ?

Je voudrais des pâtes comme plat principal
I'd like pasta as a main course
zhuh voo-dreh day pat kom pla prañ-see-pal

Je n'aime pas la viande
I don't like meat
zhuh nehm pa la vyahñd

Est-ce que c'est fait avec du bouillon de légumes?
Is it made with vegetable stock?
es kuh say feh a-vek dew boo-yoñ duh lay-gewm?

Chapter 45 Wines and spirits / vins

La carte des vins, s'il vous plaît
The wine list, please
la kart day vañ, seel voo pleh

du vin blanc/du vin rouge
white wine/red wine
dew vañ blahñ/dew vañ roozh

Pouvez-vous nous recommander un bon vin?
Can you recommend a good wine?
poo-vay voo noo ruh-ko-mahñ-day uñ boñ vañ?

Une bouteille...
A bottle...
ewn boo-tay-yuh...

Un pichet...
A carafe...
uñ pee-sheh...

de la cuvée du patron
of the house wine
duh la kew-vay dew pa-troñ

Qu'est-ce que vous avez comme digestifs?
What liqueurs do you have?
Kes kuh voo za-vay kom dee-zheh-steef?

Part 6: Traveling & Planning (Trips, Weather, Activities) – Voyages et plannifications (météo et activités)

*L*earning French often inspires you to daydream about traveling and planning trips to French-speaking countries. This type of wanderlust can be greatly expedited with some French vocabulary and phrases related to traveling and planning. From the beach to the mountains, from camping to sightseeing, this chapter will give you some practical and useful hints for planning your dream holiday.

Chapter 46 Accomodations- Hébergements

Un hôtel à prix modérés
an inexpensive hotel
uh noh-tel ah pree maw- day-ray

Je cherche un bon hôtel
I am looking for a good hotel
zhuh shehrsh uhn baw noh-tel

Une pension
a boarding house
ewn pahnsyaum

Un appartement meublé
full furnished apartment
uh nap-par-tuh-mahn muh-blay

Je (ne) veux (pas) être au centre ville
I (do not) want to be at the center of town
zhuh (nuh) vuh (pah) eytruh oh sen-truh veal

Où il n'y a pas de bruit
Where it is not noisy
oo eel nee a pah duh brwee

J'ai réservé une chambre pour aujourd'hui
I have a reservation for today
zhay ray-zehr-vay ewn SHAHNbruh poor oh-zhoord-wee

Avez-vous une chambre, en vacance?
Do you have a room, a vacancy?
a-vay-voo zewn SHAHNbruh, ewn va-kahnss?

Une chambre climatisée
an air conditioned room
ewn SHAHN-bruh klee-ma-teezay

Une chambre à un lit
A single room
ewn SHAHN-bruh ah uhn lee

Une chambre pour deux personnes
A double room
ewn SHAHNbruh poor duh pehrsaum

Avec repas
With meals
a-vek ruh-pah

Sans repas
Without meals
sahn ruh-pah

un grand lit
With a double bed
uhn grahn lee

Avec salle de bain
With a bathroom
a-vek sol duh ben

Avec une douche
With a shower
a-vek ewn doosh

Avec lits jumeaux
With twin beds
a-vek lee zhew-moh

Un appartement
A suite
uh nap-par-tuh-mahn

Pour cette nuit
For tonight
poor set nwee

Pour trois jours
For three days
poor trwah zhoor

Pour deux personnes
For two
poor duh pehrsawn

Quel est votre prix par jour?
What Is the rate per day?
keh leh VAW truh pree par zhoor?

Est-ce que les taxes et le service sont compris?
Are tax and room service included?
ess-kuh lay tax ay luh serveess sawn kawn-pree?

Je voudrais bien voir la chambre
I would like to see the room
zhuh voodreh byen vwahr la SHAHN-bruh

Je n'aime pas celle-ci
I do not like this one
zhuh nem pah sel-see

En haut
Upstairs
ahn oh

En bas
Downstairs
ahn bah

Y a-t-il un ascenseur?
Is there an elevator?
ee a-tee luh nasawnsuhr?

Le service, s'il vous plaît
Room service, please
luh sehr-veess, seel voo pleh

Faites monter un porteur dans ma chambre, s'il vous plaît
Please send a porter to my room
fet mawn-tay uhn pawrtuhr dahn ma SHAHNbruh, seel voo pleh

Une femme de chambre
A chambermaid
ewn fahm duh SHAHN-bruh

Un chasseur
A bellhop
uhn shas-suhr

Veuillez m'appeler à neuf heures
Please call me at nine o'clock
vuh-yay map-lay ah nuh vuhr

Je désire avoir le petit déjeuner dans ma chambre
I want breakfast in my room
zhuh day-zeer avwahr luh puh-tee day-zhuhnay dahn ma SHAHN-bruh

Revenez plus tard
Come back later
ruh-vuh-nay plew tar

Apportez-moi encore une couverture
Bring me another blanket
ap-pawr-tay-mwah ahnkawr ewn koo-vair-tewr

Un oreiller
A pillow
uh naw-ray-yay

Une taie d'oreiller
A pillowcase
ewn tay daw-ray-yay

Des cintres
Hangers
day Sanhg-truh

Le savon
Soap
luh sa-vawn

Les serviettes
Towels
lay sehr-vee-et

Un tapis de bain
A bath mat
uhn ta-pee duh ben

La baignoire
The bathtub
la ben-wahr

Le lavabo
The sink
luh la-va-boh

Le papier hygiénique
Toilet paper
luh pap-yay ee zhay neek

Je voudrais bien parler au gérant
I would like to speak to the manager
zhuh voo-dreh byen parlay oh zhay-rahn

Ma clé, s'il vous plaît!
My room key, please
ma klay, seel voo pleh

Y a-t-il des lettres ou des messages pour moi?
Have I any letters or messages?
ee a-teel day leh-truh oo day messazh poor mwah?

Quel est le numéro de ma chambre?
What is my room number?
keh leh luh new-mayroh duh ma SHAHN-bruh?

Je pars à dix heures
I am leaving at ten o'clock
zhuh par ah dee zuhr

Veuillez préparer ma note
Please make out my bill
vuh-yay pray-pa-ray ma nawt

Voulez-vous bien accepter un chèque?
Will you accept a check?
voo-lay-voo byen akseptay uhn chayck?

Veuillez faire suivre mon courrier à
Please forward my mail to
vuh-yay fehr SWEEvruh mawn koor-yay ah

Puis-je vous laisser des bagages jusqu'à demain?
May i store baggage here until tomorrow?
PWEE-zhuh voo lessay day bagazh zhews-kah duh-man

Où est-ce qu'on peut trouver …?
Where's a …?
oo es·kon peu troo·vey …

un terrain de camping
camping ground
un tey·run de kom·peeng

une pension
guesthouse
ewn pon·see·on

un hôtel
hotel
un o·tel

202

une auberge de jeunesse
youth hostel
ewn o·bairzh de zhe·nes

Est-ce que vous pouvez recommender un logement ...?
Can you recommend somewhere...?
es·ke voo poo·vey re·ko·mon·dey un lozh·mon ...

pas cher
cheap
pa shair

de bonne qualité
good
de bon ka·lee·tey

près d'ici
nearby
prey dee·see

Je voudrais réserver une chambre, s'il vous plaît.
I'd like to book a room, please.
zhe voo·drey rey·zair·vey ewn shom·bre seel voo pley

J'ai une réservation.
I have a reservation.
zhey ewn rey·zair·va·syon

Mon nom est ...
My name is ...
mon nom ey ...

Avez-vous une chambre …?
Do you have a … room?
a·vey·voo ewn shom·bre …

à un lit
single
a un lee

avec un grand lit
double
a·vek ung gron lee

des lits jumeaux
twin
dey lee zhew·mo

Est-ce qu' on peut payer avec …?
Can I pay by …?
es·kom peu pey·yey a·vek …

une carte de crédit
credit card
ewn kart de krey·dee

des chèques de voyage
travellers cheque
dey shek de vwa·yazh

Quel est le prix par …?
How much is it per …?
kel ey le pree par …

nuit
night
nwee

personne
person
pair·son

Je voudrais rester pour (deux) nuits
I'd like to stay for (two) nights
zhe voo·drey res·tey poor (der) nwee

Du (deux juillet) au (six juillet).
From (July 2) to (July 6).
dew (de zhwee·yey) o (see zhwee·yey)

Est-ce que je peux la voir?
Can I see it?
es·ke zhe peu la vwar

Est-ce que je peux camper ici?
Am I allowed to camp here?
es·ke zhe peu kom·pey ee·see

Où est le terrain de camping le plus proche?
Where's the nearest camp site?
oo ey luh tey·run de kom·peeng le plew prosh

Quand/Où le petit déjeuner est-il servi?
When/Where is breakfast served?
kon/oo le pe·tee dey·zhe·ney ey·teel sair·vee

Réveillez-moi à (sept) heures, s'il vous plaît
Please wake me at (seven)
rey·vey·yey·mwa a (set) eur seel voo pley

Est-ce que je pourrais avoir la clé, s'il vous plaît?
Could I have my key, please?
es·ke zhe poo·rey a·vwar la kley seel voo pley

Est-ce que je peux avoir une autre (couverture)?
Can I get another (blanket)?
es·ke zhe pe a·vwar ewn o·tre (koo·vair·tewr)

Avez-vous un ...?
Is there a/an ...?
a·vey·voo un ...

ascenseur
elevator
a·son·seur

coffre-fort
safe
ko·fre·for

C'est trop ...
The room is too ...
sey tro ...

cher
expensive
shair

bruyant
noisy
brew·yon

petit
small
pe·tee

...ne fonctionne pas...
doesn't work. ...
ne fong·syon pa

La climatisation
the air conditioning
la klee·ma·tee·za·syon

Le ventilateur
fan
luh von-tee-la-tewr

Les toilettes
toilet
lay twa·let

... n'est pas propre(ne sont pas propres)
... isn't clean.
ney pa pro·pre (nuh son pa pro.pre)

Cet oreiller
This pillow
set o·rey·yey

Ce drap
This sheet
se drap

Cette serviette
This towel
set sair·vee·et

Quand faut-il régler?
What time is checkout?
kon fo·teel rey·gley

Puis-je laisser mes bagages?
Can I leave my luggage here?
pweezh ley·sey mey ba·gazh

Est-ce que je pourrais avoir ..., s'il vous plaît?
Could I have my..., please?
es·ke zhe poo·rey a·vwar ... seel voo pley

ma caution
deposit
ma ko·syon

mon passeport
passport
mon pas·por

mes biens précieux
valuables
mey byun prey·syeu

Chapter 47 Weather - La météo

Quel temps fait-il?
What's the weather like?
kel tahn fey·teel

Le temps est couvert
It's ...cloudy
le tahn ey koo·vair

Il fait froid.
It's ...cold
eel fey frwa

Il fait chaud.
It's ...hot
eel fey sho

Il pleut.
It's ...raining
eel pleu

Il neige
It's ...snowing
eel nezh

Il fait beau.
It's ...sunny
eel fey bo

Il fait chaud.
It's …warm
eel fey sho

Il y a du vent
It's …windy
eel ya dew von

printemps
spring
prun·tahn

été m
summer
ey·tey

automne m
autumn
o·ton

hiver m
winter
ee·vair

Chapter 48 Sightseeing – Tourisme

Je désire un guide qui parle anglais
I want a guide who speaks English
zhuh dayzeer uhn gheed kee par lahngleh

Quel est le prix de l'heure (de la journée)?
What is the charge per hour (day)?
kel eh luh pree duh luhr (duh la zhoor nay)

Je m'intéresse à la peinture
I am interested in painting
zhuh men-tay-ress ah la pentewr

La sculpture
Sculpture
la skewl-tewr

L'architecture
Architecture
larshee-tek-tewr

Le château
The castle
luh shah-toh

La cathédrale
The cathedral
la ka-tay-dral

Le musée
The museum
luh mew-zay

211

Où est l'entrée, la sortie?
Where is the entrance, exit?
oo eh lahn-tray, la sawr-tee?

Quel est le prix d'entrée?
What is the price of admission?
keh leh luh pree dahn-tray?

monastère m
monastery
mo·na·stair

monument m
monument
mo·new·mon

vieille ville f
old city
vyey veel

palais m
palace
pa·ley

ruines f pl
ruins
rween

stade m
stadium
stad

statues f pl
statues
sta·tew

place centrale f
main square
plas son·tral

château m
castle
sha·to

cathédrale f
cathedral
ka·tey·dral

église f
church
ey·gleez

Quelle est l'heure …?
What time does it …?
kel ey leur …

de fermeture
close
de fer·me·tewr

d'ouverture
open
doo·vair·tewr

Quel est le prix d'admission?
What's the admission charge?
kel ey le pree dad·mee·syon

Il y a une réduction pour les enfants/étudiants?
Is there a discount for children/students?
eel ya ewn rey·dewk·syon poor ley zon·fon/
zey·tew·dyon

Je voudrais …
I'd like …
zhe voo·drey …

un catalogue
a catalogue
ung ka·ta·log

un guide
a guide
ung geed

une carte de la région
a local map
ewn kart de la rey·zhyon

J'aimerais voir …
I'd like to see …
zhem·rey vwar …

Qu'est-ce que c'est?
What's that?
kes·ke sey

Je peux prendre des photos?
Can I take photos?
zhe peu pron·dre dey fo·to

C'est quand la prochaine ...?
When's the next ...?
sey kon la pro·shen ...

excursion
tour
eks·kewr·syon

excursion d'une journée
day trip excursion
eks·kewr·syon dewn zhoor·ney

Est-ce que ... est inclus/incluse?
Is ... included?
es·ke ... ey tung·klew/tung·klewz

le logement m
accommodation
le lozh·mon

l'admission f
the admission charge
lad·mee·syon

la nourriture f
food
la noo·ree·tewr

le transport m
transport
le trons·por

L'excursion dure combien de temps?
How long is the tour?
leks·kewr·syon dewr kom·byun de tom

on doit rentrer pour quelle heure?
What time should we be back?
on dwa ron·trey poor kel eur

Chapter 49 Amusements - Les distractions

Je voudrais aller à un concert
I would like to go to a concert
zhuh voo-dreh zallay ah uhn kaamsehr

Au cinéma
To the movies
oh see-nay-ma

Dans une boîte de nuit
To a night club
dahn zewn bwaht duh nwee

A l'opéra
To the opera
ah loh-pay-ra

Au bureau de location
To the booking office
oh bew-roh duh law-kasyawn

Au théâtre
To the theatre
oh tay-AH-truh

À quelle heure commence la soirée, le spectacle?
When does the evening performance, the futur show start?
ah keh luhr kawmahns la swahray, luh spek-ta-kluh?

Avez-vous des places pour ce soir?
Have you any seats for tonight?
ah-vay voo day plass poor suh swahr?

Un fauteuil d'orchestre
an orchestra seat
uhn foh-TUH-yuh dawr-kestruh

Une place réservée
A reserved seat
ewn plas ray-zehr-vay

Au balcon
In the balcony
oh bal-kawn

La loge
The box
la lawzh

Pourrai-je bien voir de cet endroit?
Can I see well from there?
poo-ray zhuh byen vwahr duh set awndrwah?

Où pouvons-nous aller danser?
Where can we go to dance?
oo poo-vawn-noo al-lay dahnsay?

Voulez-vous danser?
May I have this dance?
voo-lay-voo dahn-say?

Où sont les ...?
Where can I find...?
oo son ley ...

clubs
clubs
kleub

boîtes gaies
gay venues
bwat gey

pubs
pubs
peub

Je voudrais aller ...
I feel like going ...
zhe voo·drey al-lay

à un concert
to a concert
a ung kon·sair

au cinéma
to the movies
o see·ney·ma

à la fête
to the party
a la feyt

au restaurant
to the restaurant
o res·to·ron

au théâtre
to the theatre
o tey·a·tre

Aimes-tu ...?
Do you like ...?
em·tew ...

J'aime ...
I like ...
zhem ...

Je n'aime pas ...
I don't like ...
zhe nem pa ...

l'art
art
lar

cuisiner
cooking
kwee·zee·ney

le cinéma
movies
le see·ney·ma

les boîtes
nightclubs
ley bwat

Lire
reading
leer

faire des courses
shopping
fair dey koors

le sport
sport
le spor

voyager
travelling
vwa·ya·zhey

Aimes-tu …?
Do you like to …?
em·tew…

danser
dance
don·sey

aller aux concerts
go to concerts
a·ley o kon·sair

écouter de la musique
listen to music
ey·koo·tey de la mew·zeek

Chapter 50 Disabled travelers / les voyageurs handicapés

Qu'est-ce que vous avez comme aménagements pour les handicapés?
What facilities do you have for disabled people?
kes kuh voo za-vay kom a-may-nazh-mahñ poor lay zahñ-dee-ka-pay?

Est-ce qu'il y a des toilettes pour handicapés?
Are there any toilets for the disabled?
es keel ya day twa-let poor ahñ-dee-ka-pay?

Avez-vous des chambres au rez-de chaussée?
Do you have any bedrooms on the ground floor?
a-vay voo day shahñbr oh ray duh shohsay?

Est-ce qu'il y a un ascenseur?
Is there a lift?
es keel ya uñ na-sahñ-sur?

Où est l'ascenseur?
Where is the lift?
oo eh la-sahñ-sur?

Est-ce qu'il y a des fauteuils roulants?
Do you have wheelchairs?
es keel ya day foh-tuh-yuh roo-lahñ?

On peut visiter ... en fauteuil roulant?
Can you visit ... in a wheelchair?
oñ puh vee-zee-tay ... ahñ foh-tuh-yuh roolahñ?

Est-ce que vous avez une boucle pour mal-entendants?
Do you have an induction loop?
es kuh voo za-vay ewñ bookl poor mal-ahñ- tahñ-dahñ?

Est-ce qu'il y a une réduction pour les handicapés?
Is there a reduction for disabled people?
es keel ya ewn ray-dewk-syoñ poor layzahñ-dee-ka-pay?

Est-ce qu'il y a un endroit où on peut s'asseoir?
Is there somewhere I can sit down?
es keel ya uñ nahñ-drwa oo oñ puh sa-swar?

Chapter 51 With kids - avec des enfants

Un billet tarif enfant
A child's ticket
un bee-yeh ta-reef ahñ-fahñ

Il/Elle a ... ans
He/She is ... years old
eel/el a ... ahñ

Est-ce qu'il y a une réduction pour les enfants?
Is there a reduction for children?
es keel ya ewn ray-dewk-syoñ poor lay zahñ-fahñ?

Est-ce que vous avez un menu enfant?
Do you have a children's menu?
es kuh voo za-vay uñ muh-new ahñ- fahñ?

On peut y aller avec des enfants?
Is it OK to take children?
on puh ee a-lay a-vek day zahñ-fahñ?

Avez-vous...?
Do you have...?
a-vay voo...?

une chaise de bébé / haute
a high chair
ewn shez duh bay-bay / ot

un lit d'enfant
a cot
uñ lee dahñ-fahñ

J'ai deux enfants
I have two children
zhay duh zahñ-fahñ

Il/Elle a dix ans
He/She is 10 years old
eel/el a dee zahñ

Est-ce que vous avez des enfants?
Do you have any children?
es kuh voo za-vay day zahñ-fahñ?

Part 7 : Money & Shopping – L'argent et le shopping

Whether you like saving money or blowing it before it even reaches your wallet, financial matters are a core part of everyday life. Having the ability to talk about money and a good understanding of monetary terms in French will be highly useful when using your French in real-life scenarios. If you are traveling in a French-speaking country, you will at some point need to ask how much something costs or have other such questions related to financial expenses.

Chapter 52 Money / L'argent

distributeur
cash dispenser
dees-tree-bew-tur

retrait espèces
cash withdrawal
ruh-treh es-pes

Où est-ce que je peux changer de l'argent?
Where can I change some money?
oo es kuh zhuh puh shahñ-zhay duh larzhahñ?

La banque ouvre quand?
When does the bank open?
la bahñk oovr kahñ?

La banque ferme quand?
When does the bank close?
la bahñk fehrm kahñ?

Je peux payer en livres sterling/en euros?
Can I pay with pounds/euros?
zhuh puh pay-yay ahñ leevr stehr-leeng/ahñ nuh-roh?

Je peux utiliser ma carte (de crédit) dans ce distributeur?
Can I use my credit card with this cash dispenser?
zhuh puh ew-tee-lee-zay ma kart (duh kraydee) dahñ suh dee-stree-bew-tur?

Vous avez de la monnaie?
Do you have any change?
voo za-vay duh la mo-neh?

Chapter 53 Banking / La banque

Où est la banque la plus proche?
Where is the nearest bank?
oo eh la bahnk la plew prawsh?

À quel guichet puis-je toucher ceci?
At which window can I cash this?
ah kel ghee-sheh PWEE-zhuh tooshay suhsee?

Pouvez-vous me changer ceci?
Can you change this for me?
poo-vay-voo muh shahn-zhay suhsee?

Voulez-vous payer un chèque?
Will you cash a check?
voo-lay-voo pay-yay uhn shek?

Ne me donnez pas de gros billets
Do not give me large bills
nuh muh daw-nay pah duh groh bee-yeh

Puis-je avoir de la petite monnaie?
May I have some change?
pwee-zha-vwahr duh la puh-teet maw-neh?

Une lettre de crédit
A letter of credit
ewn LEH-truh duh kray-dee

Une lettre de change
A bank draft
ewn LEH-truh duh shahnzh

Quel est le cours du change?
What is the exchange rate on the dollar?
keh leh luh koor dew shahnzh?

Où est …?
Where's …?
oo ey …

le guichet automatique
the ATM
le gee·shey o·to·ma·teek

le bureau de change
the foreign exchange office
le bew·ro de shonzh

Je voudrais …
I'd like to …
zhe voo·drey …

faire un virement
arrange a transfer
fair un veer·mon

encaisser un chèque
cash a cheque
ong·key·sey un shek

changer de l'argent
change money
shon·zhey de lar·zhon

une avance de crédit
get a cash advance
ewn a·vons de krey·dee

retirer de l'argent
withdraw money
re·tee·rey de lar·zhon

Quel est ...?
What's ...?
kel ey ...

le tarif
the charge for that
le ta·reef

le taux de change
the exchange rate
le to de shonzh

C'est ...
it's ...
sey ...

(douze) euros
(12) euros
(dooz) eu·ro

gratuit
free
gra·twee

À quelle heure ouvre la banque?
What time does the bank open?
a kel eur oo·vre la bongk

Mon argent est-il arrivé?
Has my money arrived yet?
mon ar·zhon ey·teel a·ree·vey

Chapter 54 Paying / le paiement

l'addition
the bill (restaurant)
la-dee-syoñ bill

la note
the bill (hotel)
la not

la facture
the invoice
la fak-tewr

la caisse
the desk
la kes cash

C'est combien?/Ça fait combien?
How much is it?
say koñ-byañ/sa feh koñ-byañ?

Ça fera combien?
How much will it be?
sa fuh-ra koñ-byañ?

Je peux payer...?
Can I pay...?
zhuh puh pay-yay...?

par carte de crédit
by credit card
par kart duh kray-dee

par chèque
by cheque
par shek

Mettez-le sur ma note
Put it on my bill (hotel)
meh-tay luh sewr ma not

L'addition, s'il vous plaît
The bill, please (restaurant)
la-dee-syoñ seel voo pleh

Où doit-on payer?
Where do I pay?
oo dwa-toñ pay-yay?

Vous acceptez les cartes de crédit?
Do you take credit cards?
voo zak-sep-tay lay kart duh kray-dee?

Le service est compris?
Is service included?
luh sehr-vees ay koñ-pree?

Pourriez-vous me donner un reçu, s'il vous plaît?
Could you give me a receipt, please?
poo-ree-ay voo muh do-nay uñ ruh-sew, seel voo pleh?

Est-ce qu'il faut payer à l'avance?
Do I pay in advance?
es keel foh pay-yay a la-vahñs?

Je suis désolé(e)
I'm sorry
zhuh swee day-zo-lay

Je n'ai pas de monnaie
I've nothing smaller (no change)
zhuh nay pa duh mo-neh

Chapter 55 Luggage / les bagages

le retrait de bagages
baggage reclaim
luh ruh-treh duh ba-gazh

la consigne
left luggage
la koñ-see-nyuh

le chariot à bagages
luggage trolley
luh sha-ryoh a ba-gazh

Mes bagages ne sont pas encore arrivés
My luggage hasn't arrived yet
may ba-gazh nuh soñ pa ahñ-kor a-reevay

Ma valise a été abîmée pendant le vol
My suitcase has been damaged on the flight
ma va-leez a ay-tay a-bee-may pahñ- dahñ luh vol

Chapter 56 Repairs / la réparation

le cordonnier
shoe repairer
luh kor-don-yay

réparations minute
repairs while you wait
ray-pa-ra-syoñ mee-newt

C'est cassé
This is broken
say ka-say

Où est-ce que je peux le faire réparer?
Where can I get this repaired?
oo es kuh zhuh puh luh fehr ray-pa-ray?

Pouvez-vous réparer…?
Can you repair…?
poo-vay voo ray-pa-ray…?

ces chaussures
these shoes
say shoh-sewr

ma montre
my watch
ma moñtr

Je veux courir les magasins
I want to go shopping
zhuh vuh koo-reer lay ma-ga-zen

J'aime cela
I like that
zhem suh-la

Combien est-ce?
How much is it?
kawn-byen ess?

C'est très cher
It is very expensive
seh treh shehr

Je préfère quelque chose de mieux (de moins cher)
I prefer something better (cheaper)
zhuh pray-fehr kel-kuh-shawz duh myuh (duh mwen shehr)

Montrez-m'en d'autres
Show me some others
mawn-tray-mahn DOH-truh

Puis-je l'essayer?
May I try this on?
PWEE-zhuh lehsay-yay?

Puis-je en commander un?
Can I order one?
pwee-zhahn kaw-mahn-day uhn?

Combien de temps cela prendra-t-il?
How long will it take?
kawn-byen duh tahn suh-la-prahn-dra-teel?

Veuillez prendre mes mesures
Please take my measurements
vuh-yay PRAHN-druh may muh-zewr

Pouvez-vous l'expédier à New-York?
Can you ship it to New York City?
poo-vay-voo lex-pay-dyay ah New York?

À qui dois-je payer?
Whom do I pay?
ah kee DWAH-zhuh peh-yay?

Veuillez m'envoyer la facture
Please bill me
vuh-yay mahn-vwah-yay lafak-tewr

Je veux acheter un bonnet de bain
I want to buy a bathing cap
zhuh vuh zash-tay uhn baw-neh duh ben

Un costume de bain
A bathing suit
uhn kawss-tewm duh ben

Un soutien-gorge
A brassiere
uhn soo-tyen-gawrzh

Une robe
A dress
ewn rawb

Une blouse
A blouse
ewn blooz

Un manteau
A coat
uhn mahn-toh

Une paire de gants
A pair of gloves
ewn pehr duh gahn

Un sac à main
A handbag
uhn sak ah men

Des mouchoirs
Some handkerchiefs
day mooshwahr

Un chapeau
A hat
uhn sha-poh

Une veste
A jacket
ewn vaist

De la lingerie
Some lingerie
duh la lenzh-ree

Une chemise de nuit
A nightgown
ewn shuh-meez duh nwee

Un imperméable
A raincoat
uh nen-peh-may-AH-bluh

Une paire de chaussures
A pair of shoes
ewn pehr duh shohsewr

Des lacets
Some shoelaces
day la-seh

Une paire de pantoufles
A pair of slippers
ewn pehr duh pahn-too-fluh

Une paire de chaussettes
A pair of socks
ewn pehr duh shohset

Une paire de bas nylon
A pair nylon
ewn pehr duh bah nee-lawn

Un costume
A suit
uhn kawss-tewm

Un sweater
A sweater
uhn sweh-tuhr

Des cravates
Some ties
day krah-vaht

Un pantalon
Trousers
uhn pahn-ta-lawn

Des sous-vêtements
Some underwear
day soo-vet-mahn

Avez-vous des cendriers?
Do you have some ashtrays?
a-vay-voo day sahn-dree-ay?

Une boîte de bonbons
A box of candy
ewn bwaht duh bawn-bawn

De la porcelaine
Some porcelain (china)
duh la pawrsuh-len

Des poupées
Some dolls
day poo-pay

Des boucles d'oreille
Some earings
day BOO-kluh daw-ray

Du parfum
Some perfume
dew par-fuhn

Des tableaux
Some pictures
day ta-bloh

Des disques
Some records
day deesk

De l'argenterie
Some silverware
duh lar-zhahn-tree

Des jouets
Some toys
day zhoo-eh

Un parapluie
an umbrella
uhn pa-ra-plwee

Une montre
A watch
ewn MAWN-truh

Où est …?
Where's …?
oo ay …

la banque
the bank
la bongk

la librairie
the bookshop
la lee·brey·ree

le magasin photo
the camera shop
le ma·ga·zun fo·to

le grand magasin
the department store
le gron ma·ga·zun

l'épicerie
the grocery store
ley·pee·sree

le marchand de journaux
the newsagency
le mar·shon de zhoor·no

le supermarché
the supermarket
le sew·pair·mar·shey

Où puis-je acheter (un cadenas)?
where can I buy (a padlock)?
oo pweezh ash·tey (un kad·na)

Je cherche …
I'm looking for …
zhe shairsh …

Est-ce que je peux le voir?
Can I look at it?
es·ke zhe peu le vwar

Vous en avez d'autres?
Do you have any others?
voo zon a·vey do·tre

Est-ce qu'il y a une garantie?
Does it have a guarantee?
es keel ya ewn ga·ron·tee

Pouvez-vous me l'envoyer à l'étranger?
Can I have it sent overseas?
poo·vey·voo me lon·vwa·yey a ley·tron·zhey

Puis-je faire réparer mon/ma/mes …?
Can I have my … repaired?
pwee·zhe fair rey·pa·rey mon/ma/may…

C'est défectueux.
It's faulty.
sey dey·fek·tweu

Je voudrais …,s'il vous plaît.
I'd like …, please.
zhe voo·drey …seel voo pley

un sac
a bag
un sak

un remboursement
a refund
un rom·boors·mon

rapporter ceci
to return this
ra·por·tey se·see

Pouvez-vous écrire le prix?
Can you write down the
price?
poo·vey·voo ey·kreer le pree

C'est trop cher.
That's too expensive.
sey tro shair

Vous pouvez baisser le prix?
Can you lower the price?
voo poo·vey bey·sey le pree

Je vous donnerai (cinq) euros.
I'll give you (five) euros.
zhe voo don·rey (sungk) eu·ro

Il y a une erreur dans la note.
There's a mistake in the bill.
eel ya ewn ey·reur don la not

Est-ce que je peux payer avec …?
do you accept …?
es·ke zhe pe pey·yey a·vek …

une carte de crédit
credit cards
ewn kart de krey·dee

une carte de débit
debit cards
ewn kart de dey·bee

un reçu
a receipt
un re·sew

ma monnaie
my change
ma mo·ney

Chapter 57 Laundry / la lessive

le pressing
dry-cleaner's
luh preh-seeng

la laverie automatique
Launderette/ laundromat
la lav-ree oh-to-ma-teek

la lessive en poudre
washing powder
la leh-seev ahñ poodr

Chapter 58 To Complain / Se plaindre

Ça ne marche pas
This doesn't work
sa nuh marsh pa

C'est sale
It's dirty
say sal

Le/La … ne marche pas
The … doesn't work
luh/la … nuh marsh pa

Les … ne marchent pas
The … don't work
lay … nuh marsh pa

la lumière
light
la lew-myehr

la serrure
lock
la seh-rewr

le chauffage
heating
luh shoh-fazh

la climatisation
air conditioning
la klee-ma-tee-za-syoñ

C'est cassé
It's broken
say ka-say

Je veux être remboursé(e)
I want a refund
zhuh vuh etr rahñ-boor-say

Chapter 59 Problems / Les problèmes

Pouvez-vous m'aider?
Can you help me?
poo-vay voo meh-day?

Je parle très peu le français
I speak very little French
zhuh parl treh puh luh frahñ-seh

Est-ce qu'il y a quelqu'un qui parle anglais ici?
Does anyone here speak English?
es keel ya kel-kuñ kee parl ahñ-gleh ee-see?

Je voudrais parler au responsable
I would like to speak to whoever is in charge
zhuh voo-dreh par-lay oh reh-spoñ-sabl

Je me suis perdu(e)
I'm lost
zhuh muh swee pehr-dew

pour aller à/au...?
How do I get to...?
poor a-lay a/oh...?

J'ai raté...
I missed...
zhay ra-tay...

mon train
my train
moñ trañ

mon avion
my plane
moñ na-vyoñ

ma correspondance
my connection
ma ko-res-poñ-dahñs

J'ai raté mon avion à cause d'une grève
I've missed my flight because there was a strike
zhay ra-tay moñ na-vyoñ a kohz dewn grev

Le car est parti sans moi
The coach has left without me
luh kar ay par-tee sahñ mwa

Pouvez-vous me montrer comment ça marche?
Can you show me how this works?
poo-vay voo muh moñ-tray ko-mahñ sa marsh?

J'ai perdu mon porte-monnaie
I have lost my purse
zhay pehr-dew moñ port-mo-neh

Je dois aller à/au (etc.)…
I need to get to…
zhuh dwa a-lay a/oh…

Laissez-moi tranquil(le)!
leave me alone!
leh-say mwa trahñ-keel!

Allez-vous en!
Go away!
a-lay voo zahñ!

Chapter 60 Emergencies / les urgences

police
police
po-lees

Ambulance
ambulance
ahñ-bew-lahñs

pompiers
fire brigade
poñ-pyay

commissariat
police station (in large towns)
ko-mee-sar-ya

gendarmerie
police station (in villages and small towns)
zhahñ-darm-ree

urgences
accident and emergency department
ewr-zhahñs

Au secours!
Help!
oh skoor!

254

Au feu!
Fire!
oh fuh!

Pouvez-vous m'aider?
Can you help me?
poo-vay voo meh-day?

Il y a eu un accident
There has been an accident
eel ya ew uñ nak-see-dahñ

Il y a un blessé
Someone has been injured
eel ya uñ bleh-say

Il/elle a été renversé(e) par une voiture
He/she has been knocked down by a car
eel/el a ay-tay rahñ-vehr-say par ewn vwa-tewr

S'il vous plaît, appelez…
Please call
seel voo pleh, a-puh-lay…

la police
the police
la po-lees

une ambulance
an ambulance
ewn ahñ-bew-lahñs

Où est le commissariat?
Where is the police station?
oo eh luh ko-mee-sar-ya?

Je veux signaler un vol
I want to report a theft
zhuh vuh seen-ya-lay uñ vol

On m'a volé/attaqué(e)
I've been robbed/ attacked
oñ ma vo-lay/a-ta-kay

On m'a violée
I've been raped
oñ ma vee-o-lay

Je veux parler à une femme agent de police
I want to speak to a policewoman
zhuh vuh par-lay a ewn fam a-zhahñ duh po-lees

On m'a volé…
Someone has stolen…
oñ ma vo-lay…

mon sac à main
my handbag
moñ sak a mañ

mon argent
my money
moñ nar-zhahñ

On a forcé ma voiture
My car has been broken into
oñ na for-say ma vwa-tewr

On m'a volé ma voiture
My car has been stolen
oñ ma vo-lay ma vwa-tewr

Il faut que je passe un coup de téléphone
I need to make a telephone call
eel foh kuh zhuh pas uñ koo duhtay-lay-fon

Il me faut un constat pour mon assurance
need a report for my insurance
eel muh foh uñ kon-sta poor moñ na-sew-rahñs

Je ne savais pas quelle était la limite de vitesse
I didn't know the speed limit
zhuh nuh sa-veh pa kel ay-teh la lee-meet duh vee-tes

C'est une amende de combien?
How much is the fine?
say tewn a-mahñd duh koñ-byañ?

Où dois-je la payer?
Where do I pay it?
oo dwa-zhuh la pay-yay?

Est-ce qu'il faut la payer immédiatement?
Do I have to pay it straight away?
es keel foh la pay-yay ee-may-dyat-mahñ?

Je suis vraiment désolé(e), monsieur l'agent
I'm very sorry, officer
zhuh swee vray-mahñ day-zo-lay, muh-syuh la-zhahñ

Vous avez brûlé un feu rouge
You went through a red light
voo za-vay brew-lay uñ fuh roozh

Vous n'avez pas cédé la priorité
You didn't give way
voo na-vay pa say-day la pree-o-ree-tay

Part 8 : Health – La santé

*I*f you are traveling to a French-speaking country, you will need to know some health-related vocabulary. Whether you require pain-killers from the pharmacy or have an emergency doctor's visit while abroad, you will likely encounter health-related situations and it is an invaluable skill to be able to speak the necessary French to navigate such issues.

Chapter 60 Pharmacy / La pharmacie

la pharmacie
pharmacy/chemist's
la far-ma-see

la pharmacie de garde
duty chemist's
la far-ma-see duh gard

Avez-vous quelque chose pour le/la (etc.)…?
Can you give me something for…?
a-vay voo kel-kuh shohz poor luh/la…?

le mal de tête
a headache
luh mal duh tet

Part 8 : Health – La santé

le mal des transports
car sickness
luh mal day trahñ-spor

la grippe
flu
la greep

la diarrhée
diarrhea
la dya-ray

les coups de soleil
sunburn
lay koo duh so-leh-yuh

C'est sans danger pour les enfants?
Is it safe for children?
say sahñ dahñ-zhay poor lay zahñ-fahñ?

Combien je dois lui en donner?
How much should I give him/her?
koñ-byañ zhuh dwa lwee ahñ do-nay?

Chapter 61 Dealing with Medical Issues / Les problèmes médicaux

un dentiste
a dentist
un don·teest

un médecin
a doctor
un meyd·sun

un hôpital
a hospital
u·no·pee·tal

une pharmacie (de nuit)
a (night) pharmacist
ewn far·ma·see (de nwee)

J'ai besoin d'un médecin(qui parle anglais).
I need a doctor (who speaks English).
zhey be·zwun dun meyd·sun (kee parl ong·gley)

Est-ce que je peux voir une femme médecin?
Could I see a female doctor?
es·ke zhe peu vwar ewn fam meyd·sun

Je n'ai plus de médicaments.
I've run out of my medication.
zhe ney plew de mey·dee·ka·mon

Part 8 : Health – La santé

Je suis malade.
I'm sick.
zhe swee ma·lad

J'ai une douleur ici.
It hurts here.
zhey ewn doo·leur ee·see

J'ai ...
I have (a) ...
zhey ...

de l'asthme
asthma
de las·me

la bronchite
bronchitis
la bron·sheet

la constiptation
constipation
la kon·stee·pa·syon

la toux
cough
la too

la diarrhée
diarrhea
la dya·rey

la fièvre
fever
la fyev·re

mal à la tête
headache
mal a la tet

maladie de cœur
heart condition
ma·la·dee de keur

la nausée
nausea
la no·zey

une douleur
pain
ewn doo·leur

mal à la gorge
sore throat
mal a la gorzh

mal aux dents
toothache
mal o don

aux antibiotiques
antibiotics
o zon·tee·byo·teek

Part 8 : Health – La santé

aux antiinflammatoires
anti-inflammatories
o zun·tee·un·fla·ma·twar

à l'aspirine
aspirin
a las·pee·reen

aux abeilles
bees
o za·bey·ye

à la codéine
codeine
a la ko·dey·een

à la pénicilline
penicillin
a la pey·nee·see·leen

antiseptique
antiseptic
on·tee·sep·teek

pansement m
bandage
pons·mon

préservatifs m pl
condoms
prey·zair·va·teef

contraceptifs m pl
contraceptives
kon·tra·sep·teef

médicament pour la diarrhée f
diarrhea medicine
may-dee-ka-mon poor la dya-rey

repulsif anti-insectes m
insect repellent
rey·pewl·seef on·tee·un·sekt

laxatifs m pl
laxatives
lak·sa·teef

analgésiques m pl
painkillers
a·nal·zhey·zeek

sels de réhydratation m pl
rehydration salts
seyl de rey·ee·dra·ta·syon

somnifères m pl
sleeping tablets
som·nee·fair

Je désire voir un docteur américain
I wish to see an American doctor
zhuh day-zeer vwahr uhn dawk-tuh ra-may-ree-ken

Je ne dors pas bien
I do not sleep welL
zhuh nuh dawr pah byen

J'ai mal à la tête
My head aches
zhay mal ah la tet

Dois-je rester au lit?
Must I stay In bed?
DWAH-zhuh res-tay oh lee?

Puis-je me lever?
May I get up?
PWEE-zhuh muh luh-vay?

Je me sens mieux
I feel better
zhuh muh sahn myuh

Chapter 62 Doctor / les docteurs

hôpital
hospital
o-pee-tal

urgences
accident and emergency department
ewr-zhahñs

consultations
consultations
koñ-sewl-ta-syoñ

Je me sens mal
I feel ill
zhuh muh sahñ mal

Vous avez de la fièvre?
Do you have a temperature?
voo za-vay duh la fyehvr?

Non, J'ai mal ici
No, I have a pain here
noñ, zhay mal ee-see

J'ai besoin d'un médecin
I need a doctor
Zhay buh-zwañ duñ may-dsañ

Mon fils/Ma fille est malade
My son/My daughter is ill
moñ fees/ma fee ay ma-lad

Je suis diabétique
I'm diabetic
zhuh swee dya-bay-teek

Je suis enceinte
I'm pregnant
zhuh swee ahñ-sañt

Je prends la pilule
I'm on the pill
zhuh prahñ la pee-lewl

Je suis allergique à la pénicilline
I'm allergic to penicillin
zhuh swee za-lehr-zheek a la pay-nee-seeleen

Faut-il la/le transporter à l'hôpital?
Will she/he have to go to the hospital?
foh-teel la/luh trahñ-spor-tay a lo-pee-tal?

Est-ce que je dois payer?
Will I have to pay?
es kuh zhuh dwa pay-yay?

Combien ça va coûter?
How much will it cost?
koñ-byañ sa va koo-tay?

Il me faut un reçu pour l'assurance
I need a receipt for the insurance
eel muh foh uñ ruh-sew poor la-sew-rahñs

Chapter 63 Dentist / le dentiste

J'ai besoin de voir un dentiste
I need to see a dentist
zhay buh-zwañ duh vwar uñ dahñ-teest

Il/Elle a mal aux dents
He/She has toothache
eel/el a mal oh dahñ

Pouvez-vous me faire un plombage momentané?
Can you do a temporary filling?
poo-vay voo muh fehr uñ ploñ-bazh momahñ-ta-nay?

Pouvez-vous me donner quelque chose contre la douleur?
Can you give me something for the pain?
poo-vay voo muh do-nay kel-kuh shohz koñtr la doo-lur?

Ça me fait mal
It hurts
sa muh feh mal

Pouvez-vous me réparer mon dentier?
Can you repair my dentures?
poo-vay voo muh ray-pa-ray moñ dahñtyay?

Je dois payer?
Do I have to pay?
zhuh dwa pay-yay?

Combien ça va coûter?
How much will it be?
koñ-byañ sa va koo-tay?

Il me faut un reçu pour mon assurance
I need a receipt for my insurance
eel muh foh uñ ruh-sew poor moñ na-sewrahñs

Part 9: Miscellaneous / Divers

*I*f you want more additional phrases ☺

Chapter 64 Liquid / les liquides

un demi-litre de…
1/2 litre of…
uñ duh-mee leetr duh…

un litre de…
a litre of…
uñ leetr duh…

une demi-bouteille de…
1/2 bottle of…
ewn duh-mee-boo-tay-yuh duh…

une bouteille de…
a bottle of…
ewn boo-tay-yuh duh…

un verre de…
a glass of…
uñ vehr duh…

Chapter 65 Quantity / Quantités

cent grammes de...
100 grams of...
sahñ gram duh...

un demi-kilo de...
a half kilo of...
uñ duh-mee kee-loh duh...

un kilo de...
a kilo of...
uñ kee-loh duh...

une tranche de...
a slice of...
ewn trahñsh duh...

une portion de...
a portion of...
ewn por-syoñ de...

une douzaine de...
a dozen...
ewn doo-zen duh...

une boîte de...
a box of...
ewn bwat duh...

un paquet de…
a packet of…
uñ pa-keh duh…

une brique de…
a carton of…
ewn breek duh…

un pot de…
a jar of…
uñ poh duh…

500 euros de…
500 euros of…
Sañk-son uh-roh duh…

un quart
a quarter
uñ kar

dix pour cent
ten per cent
dee poor sahñ

plus de…
more…
plews duh…

moins de…
less…
mwañ duh…

Part 9: Miscellaneous / Divers

assez de…
enough of…
a-say duh…

le double
double
luh doobl

deux fois
twice
duh fwa

Chapter 66 Cardinal numbers / les nombres cardinaux

zéro
0
zay-roh

un
1
uñ

deux
2
duh

trois
3
trwa

quatre
4
katr

cinq
5
sañk

six
6
sees

Part 9: Miscellaneous / Divers

sept
7
set

huit
8
weet

neuf
9
nuhf

dix
10
dees

onze
11
oñz

douze
12
dooz

treize
13
trez

quatorze
14
ka-torz

quinze
15
kañz

seize
16
sez

dix-sept
17
dees-set

dix-huit
18
deez-weet

dix-neuf
19
deez-nuhf

vingt
20
vañ

vingt et un
21
vañ tay uñ

vingt-deux
22
vañt-duh

Part 9: Miscellaneous / Divers

vingt-trois
23
vañt-trwa

trente
30
Trahñt

quarante
40
ka-rahñt

cinquante
50
sañk-ahñt

soixante
60
swa-sahñt

soixante-dix
70
swa-sahñt-dees

soixante et onze
71
swa-sahñt-ay-oñz

soixante-douze
72
swa-sahñt-dooz

quatre-vingts
80
katr-vañ

quatre-vingt-un
81
katr-vañ-un

quatre-vingt-deux
82
katr-vañ-duh

quatre-vingt-dix
90
katr-vañ-dees

quatre-vingt-onze
91
katr-vañ-oñz

cent
100
sahñ

cent dix
110
sahñ dees

deux cents
200
duh sahñ

deux cent cinquante
250
duh sahñ sañk-ahñt

mille
1 000
meel

un million
1 million
uñ mee-lyoñ

282

Chapter 67 Time/ l'heure

Il est quelle heure?/Quelle heure est-il?
What time is it?
eel ay kel ur?/kel ur ay-teel?

Il est...
It's...
eel ay...

deux heures
two o'clock
duh zur

trois heures
three o'clock
trwa zur

six heures
six o'clock (etc.)
see zur

Il est une heure
It's one o'clock
eel ay (t)ewn ur

Il est minuit
It's midnight
eel ay mee-nwee

neuf heures
9
nuh vur

neuf heures dix
9,10
nuh vur dees

neuf heures vingt
quarter past 9
nuh vur vañ

neuf heures et demie/neuf heures trente
9,30
nuh vur ay duh-mee/nuh vur trahñt

dix heures moins vingt-cinq
9,35
dee zur mwañ vañt-sañk

dix heures moins le quart
quarter to 10
dee zur mwañ luh kar

dix heures moins dix
10 to 10
dee zur mwañ dees

Il ... à quelle heure?
When does it...?
eel ... a kel ur?

ouvre/ferme/commence/finit
open/close/begin/finish
oovr/fehrm/ko-mahñs/fee-nee

à trois heures
at three o'clock
a trwa zur

avant trois heures
before three o'clock
a-vahñ trwa zur

après trois heures
after three o'clock
a-preh trwa zur

aujourd'hui
today
oh-zhoor-dwee

ce soir
tonight
suh swar

demain
tomorrow
duh-mañ

hier
yesterday
ee-yehr

Chapter 68 Days of the week/ Les jours de la semaine

lundi
Monday
luñ-dee

mardi
Tuesday
mar-dee

mercredi
Wednesday
mehr-kruh-dee

jeudi
Thurday
zhuh-dee

vendredi
Friday
vahñ-druh-dee

samedi
Saturday
sam-dee

dimanche
Sunday
dee-mahñsh

hier
yesterday
ee-yehr

demain
tomorrow
duh-mañ

aujourd'hui
today
oh-zhoor-dwee

ce soir
tonight
suh swar

avant-hier
the day before yesterday
ahvang tee yehr

la veille
last night
lah vay-yuh

après-demain
the day after tomorrow
ahpray duh-mañ

le matin
the morning
luh mahtañ

l'après-midi
the afternoon
lah pray meedee

le soir
the evening
luh swar

la nuit
the night
lah nwee

la semaine prochaine
next week
lah suh main proshañ

la semaine dernière
last week
lah suh main dehrnyair

Chapter 69 Months of the year/ Les mois de l'année

janvier
January
zhahñ-vyay

février
February
fay-vree-yay

mars
March
mars

avril
April
av-reel

mai
May
meh

juin
June
zhwañ

juillet
July
zhwee-yeh

août
August
oo(t)

septembre
September
sep-tahñbr

octobre
October
ok-tobr

novembre
November
no-vahñbr

décembre
December
day-sahñbr

Chapter 70 Seasons / les saisons

le printemps
spring
luh prañ-tahñ

l'été
summer
lay-tay

l'automne
autumn
loh-ton

l'hiver
winter
lee-vehr

Chapter 71 Colors & Shapes / Les couleurs et formes

vert
green
vair

bleu
blue
bluh

rouge
red
rooj

noir
black
nwahr

rose
pink
rohz

blanc
white
blahn

orange
orange
Aw-rahnzh

jaune
yellow
zhohn

gris
grey
gree

violet
purple
vyaw-leh

brun
brown
bruhn

Chapter 72 Measurements/
les mensurations

Quelle est la longueur?
What Is the length?
keh leh la lawn-guhr?

La largeur?
The width ?
la lar-zhuhr?

La pointure?
The size ?
la pwen-tewr?

Combien le mètre?
How much is it per meter?
kawn-byen luh MEH-truh?

Il a dix mètres de long sur quatre mètres de large
It is ten meters long by four meters wide
eel a dee MEH-truh duh lawn sewr KA-truh MEH-truh
duh larzh

Haut
High
oh

Bas
Low
bah

Grand
Large
grahn

Petit
Small
puh-tee

Moyen
Medium
mwah-yen

Semblable
Alike
sâhn-BLA-bluh

Différent
Different
dee-fay-rahn

Une paire
A pair
ewn pehr

Une douzaine
A dozen
ewn doo-zen

Une demi-douzaine
A half dozen
ewn duh-mee-doo-zen

Chapter 10 : Free Bonus Topics : + 80 tips about the French Culture

If you have a keen interest in the French language, then you also probably have a keen interest in France itself. From French culture and social systems to wondering about French food habits (such as how they manage to eat so much bread and cheese each day), this chapter of bonus topics contains some interesting tidbits about France's distinctive culture and will answer some of your more puzzling questions.

10 Do's and Don'ts for Tourists in France

An article from « talkinfrench.com »

Did you know France is believed to be the most visited country in the world? It is smack in the middle of Europe, making it an ideal tourist destination. Geographical location aside, the country is sought-after for its many wonders. France has a lot to offer, including many of the world's most popular landmarks and tourist spots as well as a legendary cuisine.

Before planning your trip and packing your bags, however, you should know that France has a very rich and unique culture. To fully enjoy it at its finest, you need cultural insight and the right dose of tourist-tact. Below are 10 do's and don'ts to help you become the ideal tourist in beautiful France.

The Do's

1. **Do** learn some basic French words and phrases.

Whether you are off to France for the weekend, a full week, or a month-long rendezvous, you should never forget to take with you some basic French words and phrases. Remember that you are in a foreign land and, while many French people speak English, you never know when a few French phrases will come in handy.

You do not need to buy an English-French dictionary or enroll in a French language course to enjoy France. All you need is just a few key phrases to get by. Below are some French words and phrases you should include in your French language kit:

- Bonjour – Hello
- Merci – Thank you!
- Oui – Yes
- Pardon – Excuse Me
- S'il vous plait – Please
- Au Revoir – Goodbye
- Je ne parle pas francais – I don'tspeak French.
- En anglais, s'il vous plait – In English, please?

2. **Do** know when to greet with a kiss and when to greet with a handshake.

When in France, you should be familiar with the way the French people say hello. In Paris, it is expected for friends to greet each other with a kiss, while strangers are expected to shake hands. Friends also kiss when saying goodbye, and it's not just any kiss. It is usually a double kiss on both cheeks.

When visiting small villages, expect to see complete strangers greet each other with "Bonjour!" on the streets; however, you will never see that in Paris or in big cities. In fact, if you try to greet French people on the streets of Paris or Lyon, you will rarely, if ever, get a response in return. No matter how friendly you appear, the French are not the type to get comfortable with strangers.

3. **Do** take time to dress up.

If you are going to France, where Paris is the fashion capital of the world, you need to kick your fashion up a notch. Never wear tattered jeans or short shorts when strolling through the streets of Paris. More importantly, never wear such clothing when dining in restaurants.

Rarely will you see people in France in their gym clothes or jeans, shirts and flip flops. They do not go overboard, but they do love stylish and sensible clothes and shoes. French people particularly enjoy the colors black, navy and grey, so you should bring some clothes with these colors. They do not use an excess of accessories or make-up, but they do bring a lot of attitude while sporting great clothes.

4. **Do** explore the iconic Eiffel Tower.

You have never really been to France until you have paid the iconic and world famous Eiffel Tower a visit. For tourists, it is a sort of ritual, an unspoken rule that you must heed as proof that you have indeed spent time in Paris. Don't just settle with looking at this gorgeous structure from afar – nothing compares to the sensation of reaching the pinnacle of this amazing structure!

Explore it all the way up to the top by taking the lifts or stairs. All in all, there are three lifts located in the North, East and West pillars which will take you to a height of 15 m. If you really want to go up all 275 m to the very top, you will need to change lifts on the second floor. If you are up for some serious exploring, take the stairs. This way, you will experience the tower's every angle and view.

Furthermore, in the spirit of today's "selfie" generation, you should take advantage of the opportunity to take photos! When you get home, you can show your family and friends all of the wonderful memories you captured. Words are no longer needed because the photos will speak for themselves.

5. **Do** ride the metro at night and take the bus occasionally.

Another must-do in France is to take a ride on the metro, ideally at night – the views are majestic at this time as the city lights are sparkling. It is also one of the best ways to feel like a local. Just remember that the metro does not run 24/7, so be sure to check the schedule if you are planning some late night travelling on the train during the wee hours of the morning. Aside from minding the schedule, you should also remember to hold onto your ticket until you reach the exit station. Losing your train ticket will prompt the Metro Police to fine you €35 on the spot. Not good!

When you are not riding the metro, you should try riding the bus as well. It is less crowded than the metro and it provides scenic views that are just as endearing as the train while on the road. Bus stops are generally all around the city, so you might as well make use of them as much as the locals do!

6. **Do** go shopping.

If you have a fortune allotted for shopping, good for you! If you visited Paris for the sole purpose of shopping until you drop, even better. The city is like a mini world full of all kinds of boutiques, including luxury and designer stores as well as sprawling chain stores. In other words, you will pretty much find everything you are looking for in Paris, everything from bargains for the budget-conscious shoppers to high-end haute couture for those who are willing to spend a bit more. However, do not expect stores to be open 24/7. Though rare, there are even some stores which close during the typical lunch hours (12:00 to 2:00 PM) as well as on weekends.

If you are ready for a day of shopping, some of the best streets to explore include Rue de Rivoli, Boulevard Haussmann, Rue St Honoré, Avenue Montaigne and Boulevard Saint Michel.

When entering stores or restaurants, you should say "Bonjour Monsieur" or "Bonjour Madame". It is the French's way of greeting shopkeepers and staff. For tourists, the greeting is a great way to break the ice and lighten the mood. Do not barge into the shop; rather, be mindful of the people around you. That way, you will feel more welcome and, who knows? You might just make a friend or two along the way.

7. **Do** understand basic French dining etiquette.

As one of the world's most sought-after gastronomic destinations, France has the most delicious, sumptuous and mouth watering food selection. Before indulging, however,, it is necessary to learn basic French table and dining manners.

Once seated, place your napkin in your lap and keep your hands *on* the table and your elbows *off* of the table during the meal.

The following are some basic food tips you should be aware of:

- Wine glasses are filled halfway, never to the brim.
- Bread is broken, never cut.
- Salad is folded using your fork, never cut with a knife or fork.
- When eating fruits, peel and slice them first.
- When slicing cheese, do not do it off the point.

In addition, coffee and tea are often ordered for breakfast but seldom for other meals of the day. If you must drink coffee or tea for lunch or dinner, you should order it after dessert, not with your dessert. Finally, eating on the go is never appropriate in France, The French prefer to sit and take their time savoring every bite when eating, Although this is gradually changing, if you want to experience what all the fuss is about regarding French cuisine, you should follow their lead.

8. **Do** bring a gift for your host when invited over.

If you happen to make some friends while in France, lucky you! Some French people love to invite guests over, although you should not expect a grand tour, especially in the kitchen. When you do get invited over for dinner or a party, remember to bring a token of thanks to your host. A bottle of wine or a bouquet of flowers make great gifts. Be sure to arrive on time, and dress up.

When seated, do not begin eating until your host says, "Bon appétit!" Keep in mind the proper dining manners as mentioned above, and the biggest compliment you can give your host is to finish everything on your plate.

9. **Do** tip your waiter when ordering in cafés and restaurants.

Tipping in France, particularly in Paris, is a different process than in America. When dining in restaurants and cafés, the tip is already included in your check, as required by French law. It is the 15% service charge or "service compris" you see in your check. Giving a little extra tip to your waiter, however, is highly encouraged and appreciated. You are not obligated to do so, but it is common courtesy. Giving tips to taxi drivers, restroom attendants, and usherettes is also encouraged. An extra tip does not have to be big – just a couple of euros is enough to say "Thank you."

10. **Do** loosen up and embrace your adventurous side while in France.

To fully enjoy the beauty France, loosen up and live a little. Even if it is your first time in the country, you have nothing to worry about if you bring with you an adventurous spirit. This is your time to explore and have fun, so, go ahead and do it! Remember, we are talking about France, one of the most travelled and loved destinations in the world. You might as well enjoy every minute of your vacation even if you have trouble finding your way around and get lost at some point. Shop to your heart's content, explore both the tourist and non-tourist spots, and, of course, eat a lot. And make some friends, too, while you're at it!

The Don'ts

1. **Do not** talk about politics, religion, and other sensitive topics

By all means, you should express your opinions. After all, French people love a good debate once in a while. But as a tourist and not a local, it makes perfect sense to stay clear of sensitive topics such as politics or religion, especially if you are not well versed in the subject matter. Rarely do the French advertise their religious beliefs and, as common courtesy, you are expected to do the same. You should also shy away from bringing up topics that stereotype the French people in a negative way.

Part 9: Miscellaneous / Divers

Try not to talk about French military or any other anti-French sentiments. Instead, talk about sports, fashion, or anything that is interesting but will not lead to an awkward conversation.

2. **Do not** complain about long waits and slow service.

The French love to savor their food, their drinks, and their time with friends. Therefore, do not expect expeditious service when in restaurants or cafés. You may be used to the American way of grabbing your coffee or lunch on the go, but that is not the norm in France. Just like Americans, French people love their cup of coffee; however, rarely will you see someone buying it to go. More than enjoying their drinks, the French love the social aspect of dining in cafés and restaurants. Because people in France are not in a rush, you will notice that service is slower, which may irritate you if you are accustomed to fast service. However, since you are the tourist, do not complain about long lines or long waits when buying your coffee in cafés or dining in restaurants.

3. **Do not** take cabs everywhere.

When exploring the city, walk as much as you can and stay away from cabs. If possible, do not take cabs at all. However, if you do need a ride, take the metro or the bus. Not only are cabs expensive in France, but they also take the joy and fun out of strolling leisurely. Paris, for instance, is a lovely city which spans over 6 miles. You can walk from one landmark to another without trouble, or you can take the metro to one Metro stop, then continue walking.

If you have ever seen the movie *Midnight in Paris*, you know how beautiful Paris is at night. And you can only truly enjoy the city's sparkling beauty and mesmerizing views if you take the time to wander through the city streets. Paris, after all, is created and designed especially for pedestrians.

4. **Do not** talk loudly in crowded and public places.

This particular "don't" is pretty universal. Talking loudly, whether in a restaurant or on the subway, is frowned upon in France just like in most countries around the world. It is not only rude and offensive, but it is also distracting to other people. Remember, you may be on vacation, but not everybody is. While it is understandable that your excitement is at an all time high, that is no excuse to babble loudly in public. When riding the metro, always keep your voice down, as most people who are riding are locals who may have come straight from work and are tired. When in restaurants, you should keep your volume down even more. French restaurants naturally have a subdued and relaxed atmosphere. Your loud talking will not fit in at all.

5. **Do not** speak English right away when conversing with a Frenchman.

One thing you should know about French people is that, while many speak English, they are not very good at it. When you speak with a Frenchman in English, do not be surprised if you are not getting a response. They are not intentionally being rude – they just prefer not to look like fools.

When speaking with a Frenchman for the first time, try using some of the French phrases and words you have packed with you. You can start by saying "Bonjour!" to break the ice, then add more French words to the conversation. It is okay if you mess up the pronunciation. They will still appreciate your effort and, if they sense that you are struggling with your French, some will come to the rescue by speaking to you in English, albeit bad.

6. **Do not** order only one dish at restaurants.

Because French cuisine is in a league of its own, you should avoid ordering just one dish when dining in restaurants. Since you are in a land where gastronomic pleasure is at the heart of its culture, you should go all out and indulge in a full meal, which usually includes multiple courses.

Make sure to set aside enough time to enjoy and savor every course. The classic dining experience typically lasts two to three hours and consists of a three or four course menu including a starter (une entrée), main course (le plat principal), cheese course, and dessert. Evening dining may take even longer as it may include five or six courses. You should know that dining out in France is not just about eating to satisfy your hunger. It is an event in and of itself which many restaurants in France adhere to.

7. **Do not** expect to have ice in your drinks.

In America, service is generally faster because people are always in a rush. Americans also expect ice when they order their drinks. When you are in France, however, it is a different story altogether. Whether you are ordering soda or another drink, do not expect it to come with ice. French people, Parisians in particular, are not fond of adding ice to their drinks, which means cafés and restaurants do not provide ice. Do not complain or demand ice. You will not get it anyway. Instead, just enjoy how refreshingly fancy and wonderfully chilled your drink is, even without ice.

8. **Do not** expect to always be right.

Have you ever heard the statement, "The customer is always right?" That is true in America, but not always in France, particularly in Paris. French people tend to stay in one job for the duration of their professional lives, which essentially makes them experts at what they do.

When restaurant staff, for instance, deem your viewpoint incorrect, said staff consider it their duty to correct you. For example, if you ask that your food be prepared in a manner that deviates from what the chef recommends, expect to hear an explanation for why the chef's way is better for the flavor of the food you ordered. I am not saying that you cannot voice your opinion or order what you want. This is just the French way of doing things, and since you are in France and not on your home turf, you might as well trust that they know what they are talking about.

9. **Do not** just stick with tourist-y destinations.

It is only natural for tourists visiting France to hit up the popular tourist spots and destinations. After all, how can you not when these awe-inspiring and jaw-dropping sights are what make the country unique? Among the first iconic spots you should visit are Chartres Cathedral, Dune of Pyla, Palais des Papes, Chateau de Chambord, Gorge du Verdon, Mont Saint-Michel, Palace of Versailles and, of course, the world famous Eiffel Tower. Once you have had your fill of the popular sights, you should steer clear of common tourist itineraries. You can experience France your way by exploring the uncommon tourist paths. That would mean heading to villages and towns where traditional French charm abounds. Get to know the locals and mingle with them in order to truly immerse yourself in the country's culture.

10. **Do not** be intimated by all the rules

With so many do's and don'ts to remember, it might get overwhelming at some point. You do not have to memorize each one. Do not be intimidated or frightened by the rules. At the end of the day, you just need to be yourself in order to fully enjoy France. The key is to pay just the right amount of respect to the culture, norms, and traditions as with every country you visit. If the French see that you are committing accidental faux pas while still remaining tactful, they will be more likely to disregard your mistakes. Also worth remembering is the fact that the French are less direct than Americans. To know if you are being a good tourist, look out for hints like the absence of agreement. Normally, that is how the French people convey their disapproval.

So, there you have it! 10 Do's and Don'ts that you should get acquainted with before visiting France. While these are not rigid rules that you are required to live by while in the country, you should see them as a collection of tips to help you enjoy and explore France to fullest.

A Guide to French
Food Habits

Heaven is where:
The French are the chefs,
The Italians are the lovers,
The British are the police,
The Germans are the mechanics,
And the Swiss make everything run on time.

You have probably already heard this description of heaven. French chefs are renowned all over the world for creating the best kinds of gourmet food imaginable. This is the reason why French people are highly appreciative of fine food, even at a young age, and take pride in the wonderful reputation of French cuisine.

What we now know to be the classic French cuisine was developed as early as the 17th century when two visionary chefs, François Pierre La Varenne and Marie-Antoine Carême, paved the way for the distinct French style of cooking to emerge. Before this, French cuisine was largely influenced by the Italians, and it was only when these two great chefs decided to shift from foreign influences that French cuisine began to take shape.

313

As of the 20th century, the French way of cooking became standardized and codified into what later became the high-level, elite gastronomic experience known as *haute cuisine*. In the 70s, the *nouvelle cuisine* (new cuisine) became popular and was characterized by a focus on fewer ingredients and more flexible cooking methods.

Today, French cuisine is characterized by creative experimentation with non-traditional flavors while preserving the usual wonderful presentation and spectacular taste,that has influenced the world and won it over.

What Makes French Food Unique?

1.The ingredients.

French cuisine is unique compared to the culinary methods of other countries because of its "herby" take on cooking. While some cultures rely on spices, the French use a vast array of herbs to create flavorful and mouth-watering dishes. The ingredients are freshly picked from the available local produce, resulting in varied regional dishes.

"French cuisine is ultimately about creating a harmonious dish that elevates the quality of the main ingredient." – Eric Ripert, chef, restaurateur and "Top Chef" judge.

314

2. The presentation.

French food is widely known to be delightfully presented. Extra care is given to ensure it looks beautiful on the plate, making it not only pleasing to the taste buds but to the eyes as well. This is the reason why modern culinary schools are highly influenced by French cuisine.

3. It is an art form.

French cooking involves a variety of techniques which can be extremely complicated and require careful preparation and ample time to accomplish. Years of meticulous practice and study have transformed French cuisine into an art form, which is why mastering it is considered by many to be the highest level of culinary success.

"In France, cooking is a serious art form and a national sport."
– Julia Child, American author, chef, and TV personality

French Eating Habits

The climate in France makes it possible for a wide array of high-quality ingredients to be produced. Everything is freshly picked and cooked to perfection. Here are the ingredients commonly found in French food:

- Meats are often the center of attraction in French meals. Beef, pork, poultry, game meats, and charcuterie (ham, sausage and cold cuts) are all favorites.

- Vegetables – the freshest and the ripest – are carefully picked and prepared. These are then cooked into side dishes or as part of the main course. Popular vegetables include lettuce, leafy greens, tomatoes, onions, string beans, eggplant, carrots, and zucchini. Truffles and other locally grown fungi and mushrooms are also widely used.

- Cheese is among the things the French cannot live without. It is always served as part of a meal, right after the main course and before the dessert. France is home to about 500 different types of cheeses, with each region producing their own kinds of cheese.

- Bread is common in most meals, especially breakfast and dinner. The types of bread eaten in France range from simple to elaborate in composition.

The Meals of the Day

While other parts of the world claim that one should eat breakfast like a king, lunch like a prince, and dinner like a pauper, the French do just the opposite. Breakfast is usually the lightest meal of the day, followed by a leisurely lunch and then a hefty dinner with four or more courses. There is usually no snacking between meals, but kids who arrive home from school in the afternoons will usually eat bread with jam and a glass of milk. This afternoon snack is known as *le goûter*. The following is a detailed breakdown of what each meal of the day usually consists of in France:

- le petit déjeuner (breakfast)
  The French breakfast is a simple fare. It usually consists of sliced bread with jelly or jam and coffee, tea, or hot chocolate served in bowls. Croissants, pain au chocolat, and pain aux raisins are also popular breakfast breads, especially as a treat during weekends.

- le déjeuner (lunch)
  When we say that lunch is a leisurely affair for the French, we mean it. Traditionally a two-hour mid-day break, lunch consists of several courses. It begins with the starter (hors d'oeuvre), usually a salad or soup, followed by the main dish (plat principal), and then the dessert. Recently, however, the trend in major cities has been to take only an hour for lunch breaks. This means company workers and students, instead of going home, spend their lunch breaks in corporate or school cafeterias. In smaller towns, however, it is still customary to have two hour lunches during which people often go home.

- Le dîner (dinner)
  Dinner for the French is a time when families get together to talk about the day and bond over food. It consists of several courses similar to lunch, starting with appetizers and ending with dessert. The main dish, usually meats or fish, is served with vegetables, pasta, potatoes, or rice. A cheese course (fromage) may be inserted after the main course and will sometimes be replaced with yogurt. Dessert is oftentimes a fresh fruit, or a delicious pastry for special occasions. Bread and wine are also present during most dinners.

The Beverages

French people like to have a round of drinks before and after a meal. The drinks before a meal are called *apéritifs* (which literally means "appetite opener"), while the drinks after a meal are called *digestifs*.

- Apéritifs
  The *apéritifs* are the equivalent of a cocktail hour and consist of dry (not sweet) alcoholic beverages such as champagne, vermouth, gin, fino, and amontillado. They are also accompanied by bite-sized appetizers called *amuse-bouche* (literally "mouth-amusers") like crackers, cheese, olives, or pâté. Apéritifs also vary depending on the region.

- Digestifs
Digestifs are intended to help with the digestion of the meal, and these usually consist of stronger alcohols which are taken straight. Popular digestifs include cognac, fruit brandies, liqueurs, whiskey, and liquor cocktails, among several others.

Famous French Foods

There are many popular French dishes that are enjoyed all over the world. The following are some of the most popular choices:

- Breads – baguette, croissants

- Entrée – foie gras (liver of duck or goose that is force-fed with grains), truffles, quenelles (log-shaped dumplings), quiche, escargots (snails), ratatouille (mixed veggies made famous by the animated movie of the same title!), bisque (creamy seafood soup).

- Main dish – Andouillette (sausage made of pork intestine), Boeuf Bourguignon (a stew prepared with beef braised in red wine), Bouillabaisse (seafood stew), Confit de Canard (duck confit), Coq au vin (chicken cooked in wine), fondue, steak frites (steak with french fries), cassoulet (slow cooked beans and meat).

- Cheeses – Brie, Camembert, Roquefort (an old and popular blue cheese)

- Desserts and pastries – choux (cream puffs), crème brûlée, éclair, madeleine, mousse au chocolat, crepes, macarons, fruit tarts, profiteroles, and so many others.

French Dining

Modern restaurant dining has its roots in French culture. As early as the 18th century, diners were being served by some of the first restaurateurs in the world. The clientele were received either in their very own kitchens or in restorative bouillons, or restaurants.

One of the most successful early restaurants is the Grande Taverne de Londres, which was created by the royal pastry chef to Louis XVIII. Other royal chefs also opened their own restaurants, officially beginning the upscale dining culture.

Here are the various kinds of food establishments you will find in France:

- Restaurant – There are more than 5,000 restaurants in Paris alone, and thousands more in other cities and towns. The most popular establishments are often awarded with Michelin stars.

- Bistro – A smaller, cozier version of a restaurant; it often comes with chalkboard menus and regional dishes.

- Bistrot à Vin – This establishment can be likened to vintage-style cabarets and tavernes which offer alcoholic drinks and simple foods.

- Brewery/ brasserie – Serves beer, wine, and meals and are open all day, every day.

- Café – The chic little places that offer limited kinds of food and often have outdoor seating.

- Salon de Thé – This is similar to a café. It serves tea, chocolate, coffee, some snacks, and salads.

- Bar – Influenced by the American bars, French bars serve a variety of alcoholic beverages.

BONUS TOPIC: Why Don't the French Get Fat??

This is a very common dietary topic, especially for women. It even spawned a series of diet guides and books such as the bestseller, "French Women Don't Get Fat."

The question that begs to be answered, however, is "Why??" French people love food, enjoy meals with several courses, eat cheeses and pastries, and wash it all down with alcohol. So, why is it that the French are not fat?

Let's take a look at the reasons behind this "French paradox."

1. "Real," unprocessed food – Unlike in America, fresh produce can easily be accessed by the French. Such items include fresh meat from butchers, fresh farm eggs, handmade cheeses, vegetables and fruits, and raw milk. Just try to compare this with eating highly-processed store-bought dinners and fast food meals.

2. Leisurely, unhurried eating – It is a French tradition to eat lunch for two hours, savoring the food properly and enjoying the meal. This allows for proper digestion and signals to the brain that you are full before your stomach truly is. Eating hurriedly, on the other hand, will trick your mind into thinking you are still hungry, which allows you to keep shoveling food into your mouth until your brain finally realizes that your stomach is already full.

3. Less low-fat, sugar-free and fat-free versions of food – Unlike the French, American shelves are filled with low-fat foods which are actually loaded with artificial sweeteners and corn syrup.

4. Leptin levels in the brain – Leptins are sensors in our brain that notify us when we are full. Most people, however, have developed resistance to leptins, making it difficult for the brain to realize that the body is already full. Leptin resistance is caused by eating

too much sugar and processed foods, which are not often consumed by French people.

5. Well-prepared and satisfying meals – Because cooking is considered an art and ingredients are carefully picked, French dishes are often loaded with the right nutrients to satiate hunger and maintain proper metabolism.

6. The Government's support – The French government makes a serious effort to ensure that children are getting proper nutrition. An example of this is the removal of candy bars from school cafeterias and replacing them with fresh fruits. At an early age, kids are already given access to healthy food choices and are educated about the importance of eating properly.

7. Eating attitudes – Unlike people from other countries, the French actually listen to their bodies when they eat and take cues internally. In comparison, Americans and other nationalities use external cues to stop eating, meaning they stop eating only when the food is all gone – as long as there is still food in the plate, they will continue to eat. The French will not do that. They say, "Ca va, je n'ai plus faim" (I am good). Saying "Je suis plein"(I am full) is technically wrong and considered a weird thing to say.

8. Smoking habits – Another reason why French people (particularly women) do not get fat is because most French women smoke. However, while smoking may result in a thinner frame, it poses the risk of cancer.

A Guide to French Food Habits

These points are not meant to assert that the French never get fat. Recent studies actually show that the obesity rate in France is at an all-time high at 12%. This is due to the emergence of a new fast food culture, junk food, and even the shortened lunch breaks. Still, the French tradition of preparing meals exquisitely is still being upheld and continues to be a source of pride for the French people.

40 French Taboos You Need to Know

FAUX PAS (fo-pa): noun. A social blunder, indiscretion, or tactless act that violates social norms, customs, or etiquette. It literally means "false step" in French.

Just reading the definition is enough to make you feel embarrassed to the core, right? How much more would you feel this way if you were the one stuck in a socially awkward scenario?

Committing a social faux pas, especially while you are traveling in France, can become a sort of disaster. To avoid committing little mistakes, arm yourself with a bit of knowledge concerning French taboos. Trust us – you will be happy to know these. Not only will you be a shining example of politeness and tact, you will also enjoy your time more as well. Now who wouldn't want that?

For starters, let's look at what is and what is not acceptable when it comes to speech.

Taboos in Small-talk and Conversations

1. If possible, it is preferable to talk to a French person using the French language. It does not matter if you speak French badly or if your pronunciation is way off. The point is to do your best. You will come across as respectful if you do so.

A Guide to French Food Habits

(Author's note: Personally, I do not really mind tourists speaking English. There could be other reasons why French people would rather speak French than English, such as a difficulty pronouncing English words, which could lead to a feeling of annoyance when having to speak English. It is not truly because we love our language so much. While we do enjoy it, we do not demand that everyone speak to us using French.)

2. In relation to number 1, you can use "Bonjour!" to say hello. If you are truly at a loss as to what to say in French, simply say "Je ne parle pas francais. En anglais, s'il vous plait." This means, "I do not speak French. In English, please." The best thing, however, is to learn basic French phrases when traveling in France.

3. Mind your tu and vous! In English, it does not matter how you refer to whoever you are speaking to – there is only one kind of "you" to use. In French, however, you may end up insulting someone if you do not choose the right "you." *Tu* denotes a familiarity or a level of closeness with the person you are talking to. *Vous*, on the other hand, shows formality and a respectful distance. Make sure to choose the proper word for each situation.

4. Conversation starters that may be popular in other cultures do not always work well with the French. These include questions involving money or personal inquiries such as "What do you do for a living?", "Are you married?", or "Do you have kids?"

Stick to safer topics such as French culture, art, food, music, philosophy, architecture, and popular events. Just make sure you know what you are talking about.

5. Never flaunt your wealth during conversations. This is considered shameless and in bad taste. Your monetary success will not be considered a sign of good social status.

6. Use the words Madame (for females), Mademoiselle (for young females), and Monsieur (for males) to address people. The French are generally formal, which is the reason why they are often regarded as aloof or cold. You can still be friendly and warm without being rude.

7. If you are in France for business, avoid droning on and on about business matters during lunch. The French believe that there is more to life than working nonstop. Sit back, enjoy your meal, and talk about something aside from business. There is plenty of time for that when you are not at a table filled with good food.

8. Break the ice with a quick "bonjour" followed by madame, mademoiselle, or monsieur. Always say *merci* (thank you) and *s'il vous plait* (please). Good manners are awesome wherever you go.

9. It is considered bad manners to ask questions about political preferences. Wait for the person to open up about those matters – do not just jump into them.

10. Praises and compliments, not criticisms, about everything French are always favorable.

11. Do not launch into lengthy talks about your opinions on French leaders and history.

Actions and Gestures

Just as individuals each have their own sets of quirks or personal issues that they take offense about, nations also have such quirks. A harmless gesture to you might come across as incredibly rude to others. The key is to take note of these cultural differences *before* you begin traveling. When you are talking to a French person, especially if you are in France, always be mindful of the following norms:

1. Making a fist with one hand and slapping the top of it with your other hand is considered rude.

2. The American sign for "OK," which is made by forming a circle using the thumb and index finger while keeping the rest of the fingers straight, can mean "zero" or "worthless". Avoid using it so that your gesture is not misinterpreted. The French sign for "OK" is the thumbs up sign.

3. Shaking hands is for formal interactions and acquaintances. If you are greeting someone familiar to you, you are better off greeting the person with a "la bise" or a kiss on the cheek.

4. Do not give red carnations as a present. This flower represents bad will in France.

5. Chrysanthemums are not great as a gift either. Also called "Mums," these flowers are usually reserved for mourning.

6. Holding an umbrella open indoors may be considered bad luck.

7. In other cultures, it is perfectly okay to bring wine to a person's house when you are invited for dinner. However, in accordance with old French custom, some people might consider this to mean you feel the host could not provide his or her guests with good wine. An exception would be if you are quite familiar with the hosts and you are bringing a good wine that you would like them to try.

(Author's note: I personally like to bring wine or champagne when invited to friends' houses. Why? So that there is more booze, of course! Perhaps, then, this custom is no longer appropriate in modern cases.)

8. Presenting red roses to your hostess can be thought of as inappropriate behavior. Red roses are an expression of love. Avoid giving them to casual or professional acquaintances as well, unless you truly mean to woo the person.

9. Bring a present when visiting your friends' or relatives' homes. Flowers are nice (except for those

mentioned above), and are usually given in odd numbers, except thirteen, which is bad luck.

10. Always dress well when stepping out in public. It helps if you do not dress like a fashion terrorist.

11. It is considered respectful for a man to stand up or show the inclination to do so when a superior enters the room or joins the group.

12. Snapping your fingers is considered offensive.

13. Chewing gum in public is a no-no and could come across as vulgar.

14. When pointing to a certain direction, use your whole hand to do so. Do not use your index finger to point.

15. Do not sit with your legs spread apart. The French consider this impolite.

Dining

Of course, this is one topic that calls for a long list. Dining is an important part of French culture. Take note of these tips to avoid social gaffes:

1. When in cafés, never complain about how long your order is taking. Part of the whole experience is enjoying yourself and relaxing. This is not the place to rush.

2. Do not only order one dish when you are dining in a restaurant.

3. Do not drink soft drinks with a high-quality meal.

4. Do not ask for a doggy bag.

5. Parisian cafés do not add ice to their drinks. Do not expect or demand any.

6. Wait for the host or hostess to say "Bon appetit!" before you start to dig into your food.

7. Place your table napkin on your lap immediately after you are seated.

8. Eat slowly. Do not inhale all of your food in one go.

9. Make eye contact as you say "Santé" to the other people at the table. It literally means you are wishing them good health and is considered polite.

10. Avoid leaving food on your plate. This means you did not enjoy the quality of the food, or it suggests that the host does not know how to serve proper potions.

11. Do not serve yourself wine first. As a proper courtesy to everyone else at the table, ask them if they want wine before you pour some for yourself.

A Guide to French Food Habits

12. If the wine has just been opened, pour a little bit into your own glass first so that the little pieces of cork do not end up in someone else's glass.

13. Avoid putting pieces of bread on your plate. Instead, place it on the table right beside your plate.

14. Only bite directly into a piece of bread if there is something spread on top of it. Otherwise, break it into smaller pieces before you eat it.

15. Unless a certain type of food needs to be eaten by hand, touching food with your fingers is strictly limited at the dinner table.

16. Do not place your elbows on top of the table.

17. Keep your hands on the table, not under it.

18. Refrain from crossing your knife and fork on top of your plate. This signifies that you have not eaten enough.

19. Do not place the loaf of bread upside down. This is considered bad luck.

20. After a course, wipe your plate with a piece of bread for the next dish (put the piece of bread on your fork first).

So, there you have it. Don't you feel more polite already? Re-read this list frequently to remind yourself how to be the best tourist France has ever seen!

How to Download the Mp3?

It's simple. Go to this page.

http://www.talkinfrench.com/phrasebook-essential-download-audio/
In case you have an issue. Please contact me contact@ talkinfrench.com

Conclusion

*B*efore I end this book and say goodbye, I would like to thank you and add a few more things.

1. **I'd love to hear from you!**

   Would it be too much to ask what you think about this book? If you can spare a few minutes, please let me know your thoughts by contacting me at contact@talkinfrench.com. I would be delighted to receive any feedback from you.

   Perhaps you can also share your honest opinion on ways I could further improve this book. I am always looking forward to suggestions on how I could be of more help to French language learners like you.

2. **I hope you will enjoy (or already enjoyed) your travel to France**.

   If you have more questions about French travel and culture, please feel free to use the available resources in the "Talk in French" website. You'll find plenty of updated articles there about all things French: from food, music, movies, TV shows, novels, and many more. Just head over to the culture section.

3. **If you are learning to speak French (or planning to), please consider my other products.**

   I have plenty of available materials on learning French – grammar, vocabulary, a study guide for all levels, French short stories, podcasts, and complete step-by-step methods. You can check them all out at the <u>Talk in French Store</u>.

And so with that, we say our goodbyes.

A bientôt!
Frédéric Bibard

About the Author

Frédéric Bibard is the founder of TalkInFrench. com, a French language and culture website, consistently named by bab.la and Lexiophiles as the top French language learning blog from 2014 to 2016.

Bibard spent several years teaching French while traveling abroad. He has since returned to Paris to dedicate his time to developing fun and helpful French language resources.

He takes food seriously (he is French, after all), but he complements it with a love for running, which allows him to nurture his passion for good food while staying in shape.

Say hello to him on Twitter (@fredericbibard) and Google+, or visit his website: www.talkinfrench.com.

French Crash Course: A Seven-Day Guide to Learning Basic French (with Audio!)

- **An innovative approach to learning French:** Speed up language learning by focusing on French lessons you need to get by in a French-speaking environment.

- **Learn Basic French in a week:** Get seven days of high-impact French language lessons with structured daily lessons, exercises, and culture immersion activities.

- **FREE audio material:** Learn how to speak and pronounce French properly and improve your listening comprehension skills.

BUY FROM AMAZON.COM

Made in the USA
Coppell, TX
12 March 2021

51628150R20197